THE STANDARDS OF CHRISTIAN CONDUCT

Bridging the Gap Between New Believer and Mature Christian

D. DUNCAN
Foreword by Pastor Ral Waltower

A course of study dealing with the standards and guidelines for Christian living. It is designed to raise the level of knowledge, understanding, and practice of Christian principles.

Copyright © 2012 by D. Duncan

The Standards of Christian Conduct
Bridging the Gap Between New Believer and Mature Christian
by D. Duncan

Printed in the United States of America

ISBN 9781619965928

All rights reserved solely by the author. The author guarantees all contents are original and do not infringe upon the legal rights of any other person or work. No part of this book may be reproduced in any form without the permission of the author. The views expressed in this book are not necessarily those of the publisher.

Unless otherwise indicated, Bible quotations are taken from the King James Version of the Bible. Scripture quotations marked NKJV are taken from the New King James Version ®. Copyright © 1982 by Thomas Nelson, Inc. Used by permission. All rights reserved; and the New International Version of the Bible. Copyright © 1973, 1978, 1984 by International Bible Society. Used by permission of Zondervan. All rights reserved.

www.xulonpress.com

ACKNOWLEDGMENTS

"A charge to keep I have, a God to glorify." My charge is to raise my standard of Christian conduct and teach others to do the same to the glory of God; God willing, I will do so.

I have been pregnant, so to speak, with this manual for many years. God has imparted in me a vision, which includes the finished work of this manual. I have enlisted and will continue to enlist the Spiritual help of friends and mentors whom I know to be believers in Christ our Savior, and I thank them for their continued support of this manual.

I would first like to acknowledge and give thanks to the persons who are responsible for the conception of this manual in me, and bringing it into being: God my Father, Jesus my Lord and Savior, and the Holy Spirit, my advocate and guide; "and these three are one" (1 John 5:7). Without God I am nothing. I thank Him for His mercy and grace towards me. To God be the glory for the things He has done in my life.

I would like to thank my family for believing in me and encouraging me to complete this work. Special thanks to my mother, Mother Rosa P. Duncan, and my sisters Carolyn Daniels and Gloria Johnson, who helped in editing the work and provided insightful suggestions.

To my senior pastor, Pastor Andre Landers, who always provides a Word in season to his congregation at Higher Living Christian Church, and Pastor Ral Waltower for his submission to the Holy Spirit of God in sharing the Word with the congregation at the Mt. Zion campus of Higher Living Christian Church. Both are mighty men of God whom I appreciate and respect for their bold, yet loving ministry of God's Word. I give a very special thank you to Pastor Waltower for his unselfish contribution to the manual in reviewing it, giving very meaningful comments and suggestions, and for writing the foreword to it.

I greatly appreciate my friends who were kind and brave enough to share with the world their testimonies of the goodness of God and/or provided character references for me. They include Dr. K. Shelette Stewart, Patricia Henry Simmons, Linda Darrington, Linda Faye Smith, Gloria C. Dixon, Charlene Famble, Gregory Thomas, Arma Boyd, Cheryl Daniels Johnson, and Lenora Massey.

A special thank you to Dr. Stewart who, in the midst of publishing, marketing, and promoting her own book, did not think it too much of a sacrifice to provide a review of the manuscript and give very valuable suggestions, a reference, testimonials, and encouragement. She is a cherished friend and trusted confidante, as well as a true sister in Christ. To my true friend and confidant, Charlene Famble, who never let me give up on writing the manual. She always asked, "Did you work on your manual today?" She is my true sister in Christ and has been my friend for over 30 years.

To all my other friends and colleagues too numerous to mention (you know who you are), who have walked with me, shared with me, taught me, traveled with me, supported me, and rebuked me when necessary — thank you for not giving up on me, and for all your prayers and encouragement.

Finally, to all persons who will read this manual, thank you for taking a chance on hearing what I have to share. You may not agree with everything within its pages; just use what you need and disregard the rest if your understanding is different.

All of us, then, who are mature should take such a view of things. And if on some point you think differently, that too God will make clear to you. Only let us live up to what we have already attained. (Philippians 3:15-16 NIV)

TABLE OF CONTENTS

Page

Foreword ix

Background xi

Preface xiii

Outline of Manual Chapters xv

CHAPTERS

1 Making the Decision 19

2 Almost There 37

3 Setting Up a Basic Study Program 46

4 Religion vs. Relationship 65

5 Understanding Christian Standards and Principles 78

6 What Happens When I Fall? 97

7 Dealing with Fellow Christians/Unbelievers 110

8 Dealing with Sickness, Disease, and Death 138

9 Pressing Toward the Mark 147

10 Epilogue 172

11 Appendix/Handouts 180

FOREWORD

The Apostle Paul wrote to the church of Corinth that his instructions to them were not to put a leash or a snare upon the body of Christian believers; rather, his intent was to instruct them properly that they might serve the Lord without distraction. Deloris does astoundingly well to present what we believe as Christians, and how we should live our lives in order to best reflect Christ as His ambassadors.

The Standards of Christian Conduct was indeed very interesting reading and will encourage, challenge, and motivate the believer to a more dedicated journey with Jesus Christ. This writing clearly directs our focus upon Jesus Christ as the reading and studying of His Word becomes the guiding principle of our conduct.

Deloris does what many new and seasoned Christians purposely avoid, and that is share her own testimony of what God has delivered her from, and how her walk with Jesus was a process of maturing. This maturation process was the result of developing her <u>relationship</u> with Christ, and not a <u>religion</u> with Christ.

In addition to one's own library collection, this book would also be a great resource for churches that are looking for a vibrant and interactive tool for New Members' Orientation.

Pastor Ral Waltower

Background

The path of a new member begins with a decision to change the way he/she lives based on an emotional plea by church leadership. After the decision is made, the person joins the church, attends new members' classes, and then leaves the class to become lost in the shuffle of people struggling to get to church each Sunday. Somewhere between joining the church and becoming a born again believer, the new member tends to get lost. There seems to be no progression of Spiritual growth and the pastor is not able to begin all over again and explain the stages of Spiritual growth each time a person joins the church.

It is sometimes difficult to determine if the new member is being sanctified and is developing a change in character as a result of the Word being received from the pulpit. If this is the case, the person is surrendering to the will and Word of God through what they have been taught, and through self-study and prayer. The person is strong enough to take the Word received, add prayer, devotion, faith, repentance, and self-discipline to it, and develop a personal relationship with our Lord and Savior Jesus Christ.

If, however, the new member is also a new believer, he/she may have trouble converting from a life of sin based on the standards and principles of this world to a righteous life through faith in Christ Jesus.

Because of this dilemma, the new member — if he is not strong enough on his own to practice Spiritual devotion, consecration, study of God's Word, fasting, etc. — is in the same frame of mind and very little growth is manifested in their lives.

This course is designed to bridge a gap between new membership, and a born again, sanctified, Spirit-filled Christian life. Persons who have been Christians for a long time may also use it as a tool to help them maintain their walk.

This study is a start for the new believer; not to teach them the Word of God, because we have one teacher and that is Christ, but to introduce them to the fundamentals of Christian standards, thereby leading them to a deeper knowledge of Christ.

PREFACE

After all of the wavering back and forth, unsure of exactly what to believe in and unsure exactly what to do, you finally decide that things just cannot continue the way they are going. One Sunday when you decided to go to church, not expecting anything out of the ordinary, it happened. The pastor said something to touch you. He spoke to your situation, and now you find yourself moving toward the front of the church. You don't feel so bad because you are not the only one moving. Several people are headed in the same direction. You fix your face toward the front and decide, "This is the day that I am going to try to change my life." What the pastor had spoken was true, and he offered help and hope for your situation. After all, you were thinking about doing this anyway. You just did not know when it was going to happen.

You mustered enough courage to make your way to the altar, and you are ushered into a room in the back of the church — for what, you do not know. Once in the back, you follow the instructions of the persons up front. You answer all the questions to yourself and to them. They tell you that you have to complete new members' classes and understand the church covenant…you agree.

Now you begin new members' class. You feel a little alone in that you do not know anyone in this congregation, but you are encouraged because certainly you will have a chance to participate in some type of ministry and begin to meet people.

But what does it really mean to be a Christian? You know from your old church back home that you join the church, you become involved in some type of ministry, and maybe you go to Sunday School. You come to church, listen to the choir and the preacher, give your tithes (maybe) and offerings, and then go home. Somehow, you still feel lost. A church full of people and still you wonder, "Is this all I have to look forward to? Why is there still this longing inside of me for more?" Perhaps this Christian thing continues with you and Jesus alone.

OUTLINE OF MANUAL CHAPTERS

A. Chapter 1 - Making the Decision

1. A brief overview of what got you to this point
2. The decision is made, now what? – Understanding the trials and triumphs of what lies before you
3. Evaluating my own belief system
4. Beginning the Journey – The cost of being a disciple
5. Understanding the process of sanctification
6. Growth – A series of choices
7. Obedience and sacrifice
8. Am I really willing to give my time, talent and tenth?

B. Chapter 2 - Almost There

1. Now that I understand what it costs, do I want to continue?
2. Coming out of the world
3. Being real with yourself and others
4. Being true to your call

C. Chapter 3 - Setting up a Basic Program for Personal Study

1. Definitions
2. Studying the dimensions of God's Word – Written, Rhemah, and "Still Small Voice"
3. Understanding commands, statutes, decrees, and precepts
4. Understanding how to effectively learn and use the Holy Bible
5. Rightly dividing the Word of Truth
6. Understanding the importance of prayer and meditation

D. Chapter 4 - Religion vs. Relationship

1. The most important relationship
2. Knowing God for yourself
3. The cry for knowledge and wisdom
4. In all your getting…
5. The search for truth

E. Chapter 5 - Understanding Christian Standards and Principles

1. Love
2. Forgiveness
3. Humility
4. Repentance
5. Denying Self
6. Developing a Strong Christian Character

F. Chapter 6 - What Happens When I Fall?

1. How do I handle feelings of guilt and shame?
2. The truth, the whole truth, and nothing but the truth
3. Guilt vs. conviction
4. Justification
5. Mediator
6. Perseverance

G. Chapter 7 - Dealing with Fellow Christians/Unbelievers/Enemies

1. Dealing with Fellow Christians
2. Who is my neighbor — do I treat everyone the same?
3. Some of the worst sinners are … so-called Christians!
4. How to recognize and avoid the Pharisee mentality
5. Dealing with unbelievers – Can I be a witness?
6. Loving my enemies – Say what?!!
7. Judging vs. right judgments
8. I am so tired of this "church" stuff, I could just…

H. Chapter 8 - Dealing with Sickness, Disease, and Death

1. How could this happen to me? I'm a devoted Christian!
2. When I get sick or a loved one gets sick, is trying to exercise my faith enough? Is God trying to punish me?
3. Call for the Elders of the church
4. When a Righteous Man Dies

I. Chapter 9 - Pressing Toward the Mark

1. If the salt loses its saltiness…
2. Meet the press
3. Hold up the light
4. Kingdom principles
5. Righteousness, peace, and joy in the Holy Spirit
6. Fellowship with God/Fellowship with Believers (and Unbelievers)
7. Welcome into the Kingdom of God!

J. Chapter 10 - Epilogue

1. Be a witness
2. True Confessions

K. Chapter 11 – Appendix

1. Handouts

CHAPTER 1

MAKING THE DECISION
(A brief overview of what got you to this point)

The decision that you made is one that could not be made by anyone else. It is a very personal decision, and the relationship that is developed between you and the Lord is very personal. He understands each heart individually. Each one is different and must be dealt with on an individual basis.

What got you to this point of decision is a realization that there is a better way to live your life. You answered the call to become a part of the body of Christ. Something inside of you wanted to know more about Jesus and what a life in Him would mean. You no longer wanted to partake of the corruption in this world caused by sin. You may have thought about making this decision previously, but something about the world's system still enticed you. That way of life is no longer appealing to you. You may waver back and forth for a time; however, you will come to see that you made the right decision.

What does it mean to be saved? Two very popular verses of scripture, John 3:16-17, state, *"For God so loved the world that he gave his only begotten Son, that whosoever believeth in him should not perish, but have everlasting life. For God sent not his Son into the world to condemn the world; but that the world through him might be **saved**."*

God gave His Son to die for the sins of the world. Jesus took on our sins in His own body on the cross so that we may be reconciled to God and judged righteous in God's sight.

> No one is righteous on his own, for we have all sinned and fallen short of God's glory (Romans 3:23). Jesus is the only man who was totally righteous, so if we are in Christ, we are declared righteous by God.

Jesus paid for our sins so we would not have to pay for them. Therefore, we are **saved** from the corruption of this world, and from God's coming wrath on the wicked.

Romans 10:9-10 (NKJV) states, "*...if you <u>confess</u> with your mouth the Lord Jesus and <u>believe</u> in your heart that God has raised Him from the dead, you will be **saved**. For with the heart one believes unto righteousness, and with the mouth confession is made unto **salvation**.*"

Romans 5:8-10 (NIV) states, "*But God demonstrates his own love for us in this: While we were still sinners, Christ died for us. Since we have now been justified by his blood, how much more shall we be **saved** from God's wrath through him! For if, when we were God's enemies, we were reconciled to him through the death of his Son, how much more, having been reconciled, shall we be **saved** through his life!*"

Hebrews 9:27-28 states, "*And as it is appointed unto men once to die, but after this the judgment: So Christ was once offered to bear the sins of many; and unto them that look for him shall he appear the second time without sin unto **salvation**.*"

The decision you made to accept Christ and live for Him is the beginning of a <u>journey</u> to become like Christ. You are now declared righteous in God's sight through faith in Jesus Christ. He will be with you and the Holy Spirit is here to guide you into all truth and teach you His ways.

I, personally, straddled the fence for a time, not really sure I wanted the responsibility of change. I was happy living in a world of sin (or so I thought). Besides, I was never a bad person. As a matter of fact, I was a very decent person. I had a decent job, a decent home, a decent character. By the world's standard, and from all appearances, I pretty much had it "going on." On the inside, however, where I thought no one could see or touch, I was feeling insecure, dysfunctional, and alone. I did not realize that no matter how I tried to hide it, how I <u>really</u> felt came out in the way I spoke, handled my affairs, reacted to conflict, and related to other people. I knew something had to change, and it had to be strong to deal with what was going on inside of me.

I used to think before I got saved that first I had to stop sinning and doing those things that I knew were wrong (like lying, gossiping, etc.). Little did I realize at the time that as I developed a relationship with Christ by reading His Word and getting to know Him, I no longer had the desire to do the things I used to do.

A change was taking place on the inside of me; one that I could not make on my own. If I depended on myself to change, I would never have become who I am today.

Not that I am perfect, but I am a long way from where I was when I first decided to be saved. I still have a long way to go and a lot to learn. I do not believe that I will ever reach perfection, but I do believe that with the Lords help, I will continue to move from glory to glory in Him.

****

THE DECISION IS MADE, NOW WHAT?
(Understanding the trials and triumphs of what lies before you)

After realizing that something has to change in your life, you must now find out all you can about this new life that you have chosen. You heard about this Jesus Christ or maybe you know <u>about</u> Him yourself through Sunday School, church, friends, teachers, or your parents. But now you have to get to know Him for yourself. You may ask, "How can I get to know someone I cannot see or hear?" Getting to know Christ is a most amazing and mysterious phenomenon because you will experience a spiritual connection to Him that has nothing to do with your five senses. You will begin to sense His presence, and eventually have a knowing of His voice and will.

> This new spiritual experience is one like you have never experienced before. <u>It starts with God, it continues with God, and it ends with God</u>. Once He is taken out of the picture, it fails, and you are right back where you started. You will again become a restless wanderer. So keep in mind that it is all about God.

The way to God is through His son Jesus Christ (John 14:6). Therefore, a close relationship with Jesus Christ is paramount. Get to know Jesus, and you will get to know God. One way to get to know Christ is through the Word of God or the Holy Bible. It has the entire plan of salvation within its pages from beginning to end.

This plan of salvation is not for everyone. It is only for those who have been called to it; only for those who can accept it. You will know if it is for you because you will have a deep yearning for it; one that cannot be quenched by the world, no matter how hard you try. There is always something drawing and pulling you, no matter how you try to resist. You may avoid it for awhile and enjoy the pleasures of the world, but somehow you are not totally satisfied with that.

This journey that you are beginning to undertake is a growing process. It goes line upon line and precept upon precept. It is a gradual process. It does not always change your circumstances, but <u>it always changes you</u>. You will barely notice the change. Others will often notice it before you do. Nonetheless, it is a wonder-ful change. No change comes without its challenges. Like working your muscles, it will hurt sometimes at first as you are learning to turn away from your past and grab hold of a new life. But as you persevere, you will find that <u>life in general becomes easier and easier to handle</u>. This is so because you will begin to understand that you do not have to handle it. Eventually, as you relinquish your life to Christ, the Holy Spirit becomes your guide, comforter and advocate.

As you begin to surrender your old life for His new life, He will begin to use you. You will be amazed at the newfound strength and peace you will have. You will worry less about yourself, and more about doing the business of God. Sounds easy doesn't it? Well, like all things, it is easier said than done.

> The hard part is not God using us or fulfilling His promises made through His Word; but it is a challenge for us to give up our old ways, renew our minds, believe that what God's Word says is true, and practice what it says.

In this course, I hope that you will learn what it is to be a Christian and, with that knowledge, begin to establish a right relationship with our Lord and Savior Jesus Christ. You will be able to tell anyone the reason for the hope that you have in Christ; you will understand the fear of the Lord, which is the beginning of wisdom; you will be able to understand the Holy Bible and use it for your decision making; and finally, you will be able to raise the standard of Christian living and receive a rich welcome into the Kingdom of God.

****

EVALUATING YOUR OWN BELIEF SYSTEM
(Pride and Prejudice)

When you begin to diligently spend time in the presence of the Lord and read His Word, it suddenly becomes alive in you. It convicts you of some things that you have not quite turned loose, and forces you to take a look at your own life. We, as a people, have an uncanny way of lying to ourselves and covering up our faults and insecurities many times. We do this because it is too hard or hurts too much to face them. If we are honest with ourselves **first**, we will find that it is easier to be honest with God and others. God knows our hearts anyway and nothing is hidden from Him. The Word will reveal some inconsistencies in our walk and show us some things about ourselves that we would just rather keep hidden.

Evaluate what your beliefs were before (and after) you became a Christian, about church in general, preachers, other races, other religions, and yourself. Did you have negative attitudes about these groups of people or yourself? Did you have the attitude that people in church were all hypocrites; preachers were out to get your money, it's all a business anyway; White people are sneaky and have been getting away with breaking the law since the beginning; Black people are lazy; foreigners are coming to this country and being taken care of by the government, they are taking over "our" country; Baptists are not saved and sanctified; or Jehovah's Witnesses don't understand the Holy Bible? These attitudes and beliefs are racial and religious stereotypes and should have no place in the mind of a Christian. Did you think thoughts like, "I am stupid and will never make it in life;" or "I know more than most and I can't understand why people act the way they do"?

Do you still have some of those same beliefs and attitudes? If so, there's no use denying it. Be honest about how you feel. We have had opinions about people and situations since we were young. We were taught to have an opinion, and we were <u>taught prejudices</u> either in the home or in our community, school, etc. We were either accepted and nurtured by our parents or criticized and talked down to by them. All of this shaped our lives and our belief systems.

Now that we have embarked upon a new life in Christ, we must face our belief systems and prejudices and know, "he says, she says, and even I may say, but what matters is, what does God say?" We are old wineskins that need to be renewed before we are able to get new wine (or new Spirit). Each person will have to give an account of their own life here on earth.

> The fact of the matter is, it does not matter in our walk with Christ what others are doing in their homes, churches, communities, schools, government, etc., as much as what **we** are doing in our personal relationship with Christ.

To evaluate what you believe about yourself and others, you should first <u>know</u> how you feel about yourself and others. Try to keep a journal to document your thoughts, feelings, spiritual growth, and progress during this new experience. Write down how you feel about yourself, church, preachers, religion in general, other races, your job, your boss, etc. Be brutally honest with yourself. After all it's only you and God here and you are not doing this for God. He already knows your heart. It is more for you, so that when confronted with the issue of church, other races, etc., you do not have to think about it to respond. Don't try to fool yourself by thinking that you really love everyone and have no issues with anyone.

The Holy Bible says in James 3:13-15 (NIV), *"Who is wise and understanding among you? Let him show it by his good life, by deeds done in the humility that comes from wisdom. But if you harbor bitter envy and selfish ambition in your hearts, do not boast about it or **deny the truth**. Such 'wisdom' does not come down from heaven but is earthly, unspiritual, of the devil."*

Denying the truth does not help you or impress God. If a person is wise in his own eyes, he probably is employing worldly wisdom which the Holy Bible says is unspiritual and of the devil. After you have been honest with yourself about different issues, confess these issues to God if you know you harbor envy or bitterness toward a certain person or group. Research what the Holy Bible says about these issues (judging, slander, etc.) and pray, asking God to remove bitter feelings, misconceptions, racist notions, or improper thinking on these issues.

Refer to chapter 11, Handout #1, on "Evaluating My Own Belief System"
Refer to chapter 11, Handout #2, on "What the Bible Says About Me/Church/ Preachers"

****

BEGINNING THE JOURNEY
(The Cost of Being a Disciple)

Getting to know Christ is the first goal of a Christian, a word whose root is Christ. I believe we must discipline ourselves to study Christ and His ways in order to know Him and His ways. When we diligently seek Him with our whole heart, He comes into our hearts and sups with us. A loving relationship is formed with Him, and we become more and more like Him. When we learn of Christ, we are learning more of His Father God because Christ says in Matthew 11:27, *"All things are delivered unto me of my Father: and no man knoweth the Son, but the Father; neither knoweth any man the Father, save the Son, and he to whomsoever the Son will reveal him."* He also says in John 14:6, *"I am the way, the truth, and the life: no man cometh unto the Father, but by me."*

> Jesus asks us to learn of Him in Matthew 11:28-30, *"Come unto me, all ye that labour and are heavy laden, and I will give you rest. Take my yoke upon you, and learn of me; for I am meek and lowly in heart: and ye shall find rest unto your souls. For my yoke is easy, and my burden is light."*

What does it mean to be a disciple of Christ? The word *disciple* means follower, student, and believer in the principles taught by someone. A disciple of Christ is a follower, believer, and student of Jesus Christ Himself. The root word of *discipline* is *disciple*, suggesting that in order to be a disciple, one has to exercise and employ discipline in the process. When I say discipline yourself, I mean that you would have to say "no" to certain things that in the past were so easy to say "yes" to without a second thought; you would also have to say "yes" where you typically would have said "no." The world did these things so naturally and it has been done since the beginning of time.

You will have to rethink and change attitudes about things you thought you knew as gospel. You will have to deny yourself pleasures that you would never have thought of giving up. For example, you usually eat 3 meals daily. Now you may have to eat 1 meal a day and fast the other 2 temporarily in order to develop your Spiritual discernment, for example. You are saying "no" to your usual 3 meals daily, and sacrificing 2 meals per day for a period of fasting.

A disciple of Christ would sometimes have to forsake friends, and even family members. It means that you may have to take a look at yourself and forsake some of your own ways. Coming out of the world is not easy. Once you have been taught a certain way and operated in a certain way so that you have certain expectations of people and even yourself, it is not easy to change for the cause of Christ.

> The Holy Bible says in Luke 9:23 [Jesus speaking], *"If any man will come after me, let him deny himself, and take up his cross daily, and follow me."*

Jesus also says, in Luke 14:26, *"If any man come to me, and hate not his father, and mother, and wife, and children, and brethren, and sisters, yea, and his own life also, he cannot be my disciple."* Luke 14:33 says, *"Whosoever he be of you that forsaketh not all that he hath, he cannot be my disciple."* These words of Christ seem harsh and against everything he stands for when he asks us to "hate" our father, mother, children, sisters and brothers. It is harsh if we understand it from the flesh. He is asking us to put nothing in front of Him or love no one more than Him. He asks us not to start without first considering the cost of being a disciple. He asks us to seriously consider whether we are able to finish what we started.

It is written in Deuteronomy 30:11-14, *"For this commandment which I command thee this day, it is not hidden from thee, neither is it far off. It is not in heaven, that thou shouldest say, 'Who shall go up for us to heaven, and bring it unto us, that we may hear it, and do it?' Neither is it beyond the sea, that thou shouldest say, 'Who shall go over the sea for us, and bring it unto us, that we may hear it, and do it?' But the word is very nigh unto thee, in thy mouth, and in thy heart, that thou mayest do it."*

We should consider carefully Hebrews 12:7-12 (NIV), *"<u>Endure hardship as discipline</u>; God is treating you as sons. For what son is not disciplined by his father? If you are not disciplined (and everyone undergoes discipline), then you are illegitimate children and not true sons. Moreover, we have all had human fathers who* *disciplined us and we respected them for it. How much more should we submit to the Father of our spirits and live! Our fathers disciplined us for a little while as they thought best; but God disciplines us for **our** good, that we may share in his holiness. No discipline seems pleasant at the time, but painful. Later on, however, it produces a harvest of righteousness and peace for those who have been trained by it. Therefore, strengthen your feeble arms and weak knees."*

> When we encounter hardships, we should learn and grow from them. Once we have endured a hardship, the power of that hardship over us is taken away, and we are not as afraid of it as before. We are stronger because of it.

****

UNDERSTANDING THE PROCESS OF SANCTIFICATION

To be sanctified means to be set apart and made holy, for it is written: *"Be holy, for I am holy."* (Leviticus 11:45; 19:2; 20:7)

> Sanctification starts when a person becomes a Christian; it continues for the rest of his or her life. It is fulfilled when Jesus returns.

When you decided to become saved, you were declaring that you no longer wanted to live your life by the world's standards nor by your own standards; you wanted to change your way of life for a new life with Christ Jesus. This is what is meant by the phrase "to die to yourself and have life with Christ" or "to die to flesh and be raised to life with Christ."

Paul writes in Colossians 2:20-21 (NIV), *"Since you died with Christ to the basic principles of this world, why, as though you still belonged to it, do you submit to its rules: 'Do not handle! Do not taste! Do not touch!'"*

He says in Colossians 3:5-10 (NIV), *"Put to death, therefore, whatever belongs to your earthly nature: sexual immorality, impurity, lust, evil desires and greed, which is idolatry. Because of these, the wrath of God is coming. You used to walk in these ways, in the life you once lived. But now you must rid yourselves of all such things as these: anger, rage, malice, slander, and filthy language from your lips. Do not lie to each other, since you have taken off your old self with its practices and have put on the new self, which is being renewed in knowledge in the image of its Creator."*

This is not an easy process. During your life, you developed habits and were conditioned to react to certain situations in a certain way. You have your own belief system which you explored, in part, in a previous section. To begin to change these beliefs and reactions, you must go through a process of consecration and sanctification. Sounds easy enough, but what does this really entail?

It involves taking a good look at "self-based/fleshly" habits and understanding the things about you that need to be changed. You may think at this point that you have yourself pretty much figured out, but the Lord will show you things about yourself that you may not even realize. Once you take a look at yourself, the next thing you would want to do is confess with your mouth faults and sins, ask for forgiveness, then pray that the Lord will give you the grace to <u>allow</u> Him to change you. Understand that you have a part in renewing your mind, but if you get to know the Lord personally by reading His Word and praying to Him, you will notice a change that had nothing to do with you.

> Your enemy, the devil, does not want to lose a candidate for his camp, so he will try hard to stop you from converting to Christ.

The devil has devices that he has used from the beginning of time and he will use these devices to try to distract you, confuse you, hinder you, insult you, incite fear in you, or do anything else to stop you. As you come to know Christ, you will become aware of his devices and will be able to avoid some of them. Christ himself also intervenes on our behalf against Satan. Just know that although the devil is cunning and has legions of demons on his side, Christ Jesus is stronger and has legions of angels on His side. When we are in Christ, Christ is on our side and we win!

The area of attack that the devil often uses is our minds. He will try to make us think all kinds of things to hinder, distract, scare, and confuse us. As long as we press into the things of God, and don't give up, we will have victory over the devil.

Don't fret if you are not able to kick bad habits right away and find yourself doing the same things you were doing before you became saved. Do not focus on your failures or on trying to kick those bad habits all at once; instead, set your heart and your mind on getting to know Christ better and spending more time with Him. As you come to know Christ more, you will find that change comes naturally. You will find you no longer want to indulge in those bad habits anymore because of your love and respect for Christ.

A good knowledge of the Word is also paramount to your sanctification and developing a personal relationship with Christ. In it you will find all you need to be transformed into the likeness of Christ, because you will understand His ways and His standard of living. Believe me, once you know Him, you will want to be like Him.

****

GROWTH – A SERIES OF CHOICES

Paul states in Romans 7:15-19 (NIV), *"I do not understand what I do. For what I want to do I do not do, but what I hate I do. And if I do what I do not want to do, I agree that the law is good. As it is, it is no longer I myself who do it, but it is sin living in me. I know that nothing good lives in me, that is, in my sinful nature. For I have the desire to do what is good, but I cannot carry it out. For what I do is not the good I want to do; no, the evil I do not want to do—this I keep on doing."*

In this journey of coming out of the world and conforming to the will of Christ, you will find as Paul discovered that you want to do good, but you keep on doing what is not right. Do not be discouraged when this happens. The very fact that you recognize that you have done wrong is progress. Before your decision to live a righteous life, you did not even notice when you did wrong. As a matter of fact, you did not consider that what you did was actually wrong. It was not wrong according to the world's standard or your own standard.

Now that you have become saved, <u>you recognize wrong</u>. You were **convicted** (recognized as guilty of a sin) in your conscience. This in itself means progress. So don't be too hard on yourself. This is the first step to overcoming sin.

Paul states further in Romans 7:21-23 (NIV), *"...I find this law at work: When I want to do good, evil is right there with me. For in my inner being I delight in God's law; but I see another **law at work in the members of my body**, waging war against **the law of my mind** and making me a prisoner of the law of sin at work **within my members**."*

He continues in Romans 8:3-5 (NIV), *"Those who live according to the sinful nature have their minds set on what that nature desires; but **those who live in accordance with the Spirit have their minds set on what the Spirit desires**."*

He states in Galatians 5:16, *"Walk in the Spirit, and ye shall not fulfill the lust of the flesh."*

> It is clear from Paul's explanation that there are two laws or two forces that are at work within us; the Spirit and the <u>sinful nature (or flesh)</u> which wars against the Spirit. <u>We must train ourselves and renew our minds to follow after the Spirit.</u>

It is written in Ephesians 4:22-32 (NIV), *"You were taught, with regard to your former way of life, to **put off your old self**, which is being corrupted by its deceitful* *desires; to be made new in the attitude of your minds; and to **put on the new self**, created to be like God in true righteousness and holiness.*

"Therefore each of you must put off falsehood and speak truthfully to your neighbor, for we are all members of one body. 'In your anger do not sin': Do not let the sun go down while you are still angry, and do not give the devil a foothold. He who has been stealing must steal no longer, but must work, doing something useful with his own hands, that he may have something to share with those in need.

"Do not let any unwholesome talk come out of your mouths, but only what is helpful for building others up according to their needs, that it may benefit those who listen. And do not grieve the Holy Spirit of God, with whom you were sealed for the day of redemption. Get rid of all bitterness, rage and anger, brawling and slander, along with every form of malice. Be kind and compassionate to one another, forgiving each other, just as in Christ God forgave you."

You might wonder how a person recognizes the Spirit in order to follow after Him. First and foremost, it is important to study the Word because God's will is His Word. The Holy Spirit will lead us and guide us if we are tuned in to Him. Have you ever regretted doing or saying something and say to yourself "Something told me not to do it or say it"? That "something", guiding you and protecting you, most likely, is the Holy Spirit.

You must, however, test your thoughts to see if they are from God. God's Spirit will never tell you to do something that is against His Word. So when you receive a thought, test it against God's Word to see if it is from Him. Ask yourself, is this thought in agreement with God's Word? Does it show wisdom from above? Is it *"...pure; then peace-loving, considerate, submissive, full of mercy and good fruit, impartial and sincere"*? If not, discard the thought (2 Corinthians 10:5 and James 3:17-NIV).

As you mature in the Spirit, it will become easier to recognize His voice. Be patient with yourself, learn what the Bible says, and always pray in the Spirit for the Lord to show you the way.

****

OBEDIENCE AND SACRIFICE

In order to have a discussion on the subject of obedience and sacrifice, we would have to explore the reason for being obedient and making sacrifices. Obedience to what or to whom? What kind of sacrifices? If Christ made the ultimate sacrifice on the cross, what am I required to sacrifice?

Well, when we decided to die to our old way of life and have a new life in Christ, we took on a new role in life and we let go of some old ways and interests. We were given a gift of salvation and righteousness. We must learn how to handle the gift and not abuse it.

<u>First, we were given the gift of salvation</u>, and we accepted the gift by accepting Jesus Christ into our lives. Salvation is a free gift, but to be born again takes effort. Jesus says in John 3:3, *"Verily, verily, I say unto thee, except a man be born again, he cannot see the kingdom of God."*

Our old nature, which is sinful and dark, must be transformed into a new divine nature, which is full of truth and light. We at one time offered the parts of our bodies in slavery to sin (fornication — which is sex outside of marriage — adultery, lying, orgies, excessive drug use, excessive alcohol use, cheating, extortion, etc.; these are activities of the old nature). What benefit did we get from these things? A temporary feeling of ecstasy or power? There is a downside to these temporary highs, such as: prison, unwanted divorce, unwanted pregnancies, sickness and disease, loss of a job or a relationship, risk of life. There is a better way!

Galatians 5:19-25 states, *"Now the works of the flesh are manifest, which are these; adultery, fornication, uncleanness, lasciviousness, Idolatry, witchcraft, hatred, variance, emulations, wrath, strife, seditions, heresies, Envyings, murders, drunkenness, revellings, and such like: of the which I tell you before, as I have also told you in time past, that they which do such things shall not inherit the kingdom of God. But the fruit of the Spirit is love, joy, peace, longsuffering, gentleness, goodness, faith, meekness, temperance: against such there is no law. And they that are Christ's have crucified the flesh with the affections and lusts. If we live in the Spirit, let us also walk in the Spirit."*

When Jesus said in Luke 9:23, *"If any man will come after me, let him deny himself, and take up his cross daily, and follow me,"* He was referring to sacrificing the ways of our old nature. Our cross is "us." There is a sacrifice of our old self and old ways for our new self and His way. Just as Jesus was crucified on the cross and rose to life on the third day, we must crucify our old way of life and our sinful nature (our flesh) on the cross, die to that old way, and be raised to life in Christ, thus, be born again.

LIVING AS CHILDREN OF THE LIGHT

Ephesians 4:22-24

1. PUT OFF OLD SELF
(Being corrupted by its deceitful desires)

2. BE MADE NEW IN THE ATTITUDE OF YOUR MIND

3. PUT ON NEW SELF
(Created to be like God in true righteousness and holiness)

    <u>Second, we were given the gift of righteousness through Christ</u>. Some may say that the two gifts are synonymous. Man was always considered corrupt and unrighteous. God gave His people the Law of Moses to show them <u>how to live right</u>. No one was declared righteous, however, by keeping the law because no one kept the law. Jesus was sent to us to fulfill the law and He was the only one who could do it. We were made righteous through the atoning work of Jesus Christ, and now we have righteousness apart from keeping the law that comes through faith in Jesus Christ.
    Only Jesus is perfectly righteous, so in order to become and stay righteous before God, we must live in and be obedient to Christ. The Holy Bible speaks of becoming

slaves to righteousness. In doing this we will be progressively righteous and sanctified through the truth.

Romans 12:1-2 says, *"I beseech you therefore, brethren, by the mercies of God, that ye present your bodies a living sacrifice, holy, acceptable unto God, which is your reasonable service. And be not conformed to this world: but be ye transformed by the renewing of your mind, that ye may prove what is that good, and acceptable, and perfect, will of God."*

1 Corinthians 6:19-20 says, *"What? Know ye not that your body is the temple of the Holy Ghost which is in you, which ye have of God, and ye are not your own? For ye are bought with a price: therefore glorify God in your body, and in your spirit, which are God's."*

Please see chapter 11, handout # 3 and 4 – Putting off the old self/Putting on the new.

****

AM I REALLY WILLING TO GIVE MY TIME, TALENT, AND TENTH?

<u>My Time:</u>

Giving ourselves over to Christ involves, as stated before, sacrifices of some things we once had and some activities in which we once participated. An example would be that in the mornings we may like to sleep until the alarm clock goes off, say about 6:00 am, then get up, get dressed for work and leave the house. Now that we are Christians, we may have to sacrifice some sleep time and get up at 4:00 or 5:00 to spend the first hours of the day in devotion to God (praying, reading the Bible, meditating on His Word). This sacrifice of time is for our own benefit to make sure we are learning more and more about God and His son Jesus Christ. *"Draw nigh to God, and he will draw nigh to you"* (James 4:8). We are communing with Him and being transformed in the process, even if we don't see it immediately.

We also give of our time in service to other people. Sometimes we don't realize how much of our time is dedicated to ourselves and our families. Obviously, we have to work, we have to take care of our families; we must do what is necessary for our survival. What we may fail to see clearly is that by not spending time with God and in His service, we are hurting ourselves and our families. As Christians, we are taken care of by the Spirit, and what is done, is done in the Spirit.

The Spirit searches our hearts and minds and intercedes for us to God (Romans 8:26-27). In all of our doing for ourselves and for our families, we should take a portion of the time — however small — to care for, think of, pray for, call, or do things for other people. Endeavor to show kindness in some way to someone outside your home on a regular basis. In this we are fulfilling the command to love our neighbors as ourselves and God is pleased with us.

> First give God your time, preferably your **first** amount of time in the mornings, then give of your time to the service of others just as you give time to yourself and your family. It is a worthy sacrifice that has an abundance of return benefits and blessings.

My Talent:

Paul speaks of different kinds of Spiritual Gifts in 1 Corinthians 12. He says there are different gifts, but the same God gives them to us. God allows us to have Spiritual gifts and gives them to each as He decides.

As we get closer to God, we are able to see our gifts in Him. We are able to use our gifts to build up Christ's church. Paul says in 1 Corinthians 12:27-28, *"Now ye are the body of Christ, and members in particular. And God hath set some in the church, first apostles, secondarily prophets, thirdly teachers, after that miracles, then gifts of healings, helps, governments, diversities of tongues."* All are used for the edification of the Kingdom of God. When you discover what your gifts are, the next question is "How can I use my gifts and talents for Christ?" This question is answered while we are in study and meditation in the Word of God and spending time with Christ. You may not know everything all at once, but as you spend time with Him, you will have certain impressions of what is important to you and what you have a passion for. If you think your passion is in a particular area, but later find out that it really wasn't for you, don't be discouraged. Continue to seek God, and you will find out where your gifts and talents are most needed.

Jesus gave the charge to His disciples to *"Go ye therefore, and teach all nations, baptizing them in the name of the Father, and of the Son, and of the Holy Ghost: Teaching them to observe all things whatsoever I have commanded you: and, lo, I am with you alway, even unto the end of the world. Amen"* (Matthew 28:19-20). This is called "The Great Commission." It is Kingdom business. As the Body of Christ, we all have the same mission.

In order to do this, we must be willing to give of ourselves, our talents, and our time. This is sometimes a big sacrifice when we have so much going on in our lives. Our lives, however, will be so much more enriched if we do these things, and we will be transformed into Christ's ambassadors by first <u>being</u> what He has called us to be, then <u>doing</u> what He has called us to do. Make time for Christ in your life and use your talents and gifts for Him; you will not regret it.

<u>My Tenth</u>:

Paul speaks in 1 Corinthians 16:1-2 (NIV) about collections for God's people. He instructs the Galatians, *"On the first day of every week, each one of you should set aside a sum of money in keeping with your income [the biblical standard is the tithe], saving it up, so that when I come, no collections will have to be made."* He will then take these collections and give them to the brothers in need in Jerusalem.

Paul says of the Macedonian churches, *"And now, brothers, we want you to know about the grace that God has given the Macedonian churches. Out of the most severe trial, their <u>overflowing joy</u> and their <u>extreme poverty welled up in rich generosity</u>. For I testify that <u>they gave as much as they were able, and even beyond their ability</u>. <u>Entirely on their own</u>, they urgently pleaded with us for the privilege of sharing in this service to the saints. And they did not do as we expected, but <u>they gave themselves first to the Lord, and then to us in keeping with God's will</u>"* (2 Corinthians 8:1-5-NIV, emphasis mine).

When we give, it may be a sacrifice at times, but God remembers us and we will have all we need. Give yourself first to the Lord, then to others and it will be a privilege to give money.

Now let's talk a little more about the subject of tithing. Remember that the word *tithe*, when interpreted, means a tenth. Some say that tithing is an Old Testament law and we are no longer under the law, but under grace. This is partially true. The fact of the matter is that tithing was introduced over 430 years before the law.

The first incidence of giving a tenth was with Abraham in Genesis 14:17-20. Abraham gave Melchizedek, king of Salem, **a tenth** of everything he recovered in his defeat of Kedorlaomer, king of Elam, and the kings allied with him.

Secondly, Jacob made a vow to the Lord in Genesis 28:20-22 saying, *"If God will be with me, and will keep me in this way that I go, and will give me bread to eat, and raiment to put on, So that I come again to my father's house in peace; then shall the LORD be my God: and this stone, which I have set for a pillar, shall be God's house: and of all that thou shalt give me I will surely give **the tenth** unto thee."*

In the New Testament, Jesus spoke to the teachers of the law and the Pharisees. He called them hypocrites because they tithed of their treasures, mint and cumin, but neglected the more important matters of the law — mercy and faith. He said they should have done the one, **without leaving the other undone** (Matthew 23:23).

> Giving for the edification of God's house and Kingdom is not negated with the new covenant. It is true, people are no longer under the written law (old covenant); tithing is simply a standard of giving based on biblical practices.

Paul says in 2 Corinthians 8:12, *"For if there be first a willing mind, it is accepted according to that a man hath, and not according to that he hath not."* He says further in chapter 9, verses 6-8, *"But this I say, He which soweth sparingly shall reap also sparingly; and he which soweth bountifully shall reap also bountifully. Every man according as he purposeth in his heart, so let him give; not grudgingly, or of necessity: for God loveth a cheerful giver. And God is able to make all grace abound toward you; that ye, always having all sufficiency in all things, may abound to every good work."*

This is a profound statement because it says if we give, we will have grace for all we need at all times. We will abound in every good work! Thus, giving is a service to God's people and is an assurance that we will have all we need.

Do not, however, be pressured into giving by anyone. We are not to give under compulsion, according to Paul. Therefore, if anyone, be it a preacher, prophet, tele-evangelist, etc. compels you to give and you have not purposed in your heart to give, do not do it; this is giving under compulsion. Give if you are led by the Holy Spirit to give. Give cheerfully when you do it. Sometimes it may be a great sacrifice, but let it be because you were led to give, not because some man or woman made you feel like you had to give. Giving willingly to God and in His service will allow us to reap many rewards. Are you really willing to give your time, talent and tenth for the edification of the Kingdom of God?

REVIEW

MAKING THE DECISION

1. What thoughts do you recall having about church before you decided to make a commitment to Jesus Christ?
   _____
   _____

2. What are some of your old habits that you recognize as harmful to your living a new life in Christ?
   _____
   _____

3. What is your understanding of the words *disciple, discipline* (give examples)?
   _____
   _____

4. What is meant by sanctification?
   _____
   _____

5. After evaluating your belief system, what changes are you willing to make to allow Christ to align your thoughts with His thoughts?
   _____
   _____

6. List some of your gifts and talents that can be used in living for Christ:
   _____
   _____

7. In what ways will you now give of your time, talent, and tenth?
   _____
   _____

CHAPTER 2

ALMOST THERE
(Now that I understand what it costs, do I want to continue?)

Jesus says in Luke 14:28-35 (NIV), *"Suppose one of you wants to build a tower. Will he not first sit down and estimate the cost to see if he has enough money to complete it? For if he lays the foundation and is not able to finish it, everyone who sees it will ridicule him, saying, 'this fellow began to build and was not able to finish.'*

"Or suppose a king is about to go to war against another king. Will he not first sit down and consider whether he is able with ten thousand men to oppose the one coming against him with twenty thousand. If he is not able, he will send a delegation while the other is still a long way off and will ask for terms of peace. In the same way, any of you who does not give up everything he has cannot be my disciple.

"Salt is good, but if it loses its saltiness, how can it be made salty again? It is fit neither for the soil nor for the manure pile; it is thrown out. He who has ears to hear let him hear."

The point that is being made is to carefully consider what you are about to do before you do it, or you will not be effective in what you do. Also, do not start something you are not able to finish. Being a disciple of Christ is a big undertaking. It can and will change your life. As a matter of fact, it will no longer be your life (or a self life), it will be a life totally committed to the cause of Christ.

> Jesus said in Luke 9:62, *"No man, having put his hand to the plough, and looking back, is fit for the kingdom of God."*

This exchange of self life for divine life is not done overnight. It is not as complicated as it sounds, and Jesus is not just being selfish by wanting everything you have. He knows us individually and knows what is <u>best for us</u>. He knows what it will take to <u>fulfill us and give us life</u>. You will not regret this new life once it is achieved. I know of no one who was really sincere and desired salvation, who has ever said "I wish I had never gotten saved." Once you have truly given your life to Christ, you realize that you can't go back. You may fall or sin and be riddled with such guilt that you feel you can't be forgiven, but you will always have a pull within you to come back to Christ. If you confess and repent, you will be forgiven as you forgive.

Just understand and know that your ways will not change immediately, and Jesus knows that you will stumble and fall in the process. It is important to know that He helps us in our infirmities. All we need to do is cry out to Him. Again, instead of focusing on trying to change your wicked ways, just focus on getting to know all you can about Christ. Study your Bible, meditate on the Word, pray, and press. Change will come automatically and naturally. You won't even realize when it happens. One day you will look back over your life and say something like, "Hmmm, that doesn't bother me the way it used to." Or "I know that I am going through this trial, but I feel peace instead of grief and fear."

You must decide, before you begin, whom you will serve. Will you serve the world, idols, yourself, or God? Joshua said to the Israelites when they crossed over the Jordan, *"If it seem evil unto you to serve the LORD, choose you this day whom ye will serve; whether the gods which your fathers served that were on the other side of the flood, or the gods of the Amorites, in whose land ye dwell: but as for me and my house, we will serve the LORD"* (Joshua 24:15).

> Elijah asked the people of Israel in 1 Kings 18:21 "How long halt ye between two opinions? If the LORD be God, follow him: but if Baal, then follow him. And the people answered him not a word."

Those of you who are straddling the fence — not quite evil and not quite good; not committing "big" sins like murder, stealing or adultery, but harboring anger, bitterness, deception, and resentments in your heart; you're not a bad person, but you are not saved; or you profess to be saved, but you are not given to prayer, fasting, studying His word, meditation, righteous works — sit down and have a sincere talk with yourself. Then make a decision of whom you will serve and how you will live the rest of your life. Give yourself wholeheartedly to what you decide and by all means,

JUMP OFF THE FENCE-to one side or the other!

COMING OUT OF THE WORLD

(THE BATTLE BEGINS)

It seems that while you were in the world, things were not this complicated. It seems like you lived life without this much thought. Whatever you had in mind to do, that's what you did, based on your own intellectual decisions and what you thought was best. Now it is less important what you think, and more important what the Lord's will is. You must be more interested in knowing about Jesus and what He would say and do in different situations. Why? Because it <u>will</u> change your life.

I began my quest to know Jesus for myself because I was not convinced by the teachings I had heard previously that Jesus was real. I was not convinced that the stories I had heard about Him were true. So I went on somewhat of a fact-finding mission to see for myself if all I had heard was true. What a wonderful journey! It was not an easy journey. I was bewildered, in wonder, tried to almost the breaking point, encouraged most of the time, but discouraged at times, misunderstood, lonely at times, and at times I thought I did not want to continue.

However I did not give up. I came to understand that my trials and pains came from the self in me; the self that did not want to know Christ, the one that wanted to have things done my way. It took my understanding of <u>the flesh</u> — the physical body along with its needs and limitations, as opposed to the soul — mind, will and emotion, and <u>dying to self</u> to really appreciate what this new life could do for me. I understood that the flesh in me wanted nothing to do with God or His Son. I understood that God is Spirit; Spirit and flesh are in constant conflict with each other.

I understood this when I studied from scripture that in my natural self (flesh), I could not accept and understand the things of the Spirit as stated in 1 Corinthians 2:14, *"But the natural man receiveth not the things of the Spirit of God: for they are foolishness unto him: neither can he know them, because they are spiritually discerned."*

Galatians 5:17 (NIV) says, *"For the flesh desires what is contrary to the Spirit, and the Spirit what is contrary to the flesh. They are in conflict with each other, so that you are not to do whatever you want."*

I learned according to Romans 8:5-9 (NIV, emphasis mine), *"Those who live according to the flesh have their minds set on what the flesh desires; but those who live in accordance with the Spirit have their minds set on what the Spirit desires.*

The mind governed by the flesh is death, but the mind governed by the Spirit is life and peace. The mind governed by the flesh is hostile to God; it does not submit *to God's law, nor can it do so. Those who are in the realm of the flesh <u>cannot</u> please God. You, however, are not in the realm of the flesh but are in the realm of the Spirit, **if** indeed the Spirit of God lives in you. And if anyone does not have the Spirit of Christ, they do not belong to Christ."*

That last statement pricked my spirit and I thought, "If I continue to live according to my own natural, fleshly self, and do not change to live in the realm of the Spirit, I do not even belong to Christ!"

Once I learned the reason for my struggle with knowing Christ, I was able to accept why I was going through the things I went through. I was not really willing to give up the things of the world and come out of it because that was all I knew.

> According to 1 John 2:15-16, *"Love not the world, neither the things that are in the world. If any man love the world, the love of the Father is not in him. For all that is in the world, the lust of the flesh, and the lust of the eyes, and the pride of life, is not of the Father, but is of the world."*

If I remained in the flesh and did not try to understand the things of the Spirit, I could not understand what God had for me in this life for it states in 1 Corinthians 2:10-12, *"The Spirit searcheth all things, yea, the deep things of God. For what man knoweth the things of a man, save the spirit of man which is in him? Even so the things of God knoweth no man, but the Spirit of God. Now we have received, not the spirit of the world, but the spirit which is of God;* **that we might know the things that are freely given to us of God***, (emphasis mine)*. The more I understood the things of the Spirit, the more I accepted these things and embraced the Spirit that God placed inside of me when I accepted Christ.

We have a lot to learn about the things of the Spirit so that the Spirit of Christ can go to work in our lives. Let us begin to be true learners and disciples of Christ so that we may know and appreciate what <u>He has for us</u>. I believe that if a person does not <u>realize </u>what they have, they cannot <u>appreciate</u> what they have and may even abuse it. To appreciate Christ and what He has for us, let us first understand Him and what He is all about. Then we will be true disciples of Christ and we will be equipped and well able to share Him with others.

Romans 8:10-11 says, *"And if Christ be in you, the body is dead because of sin; but the Spirit is life because of righteousness. But if the Spirit of him that raised up Jesus from the dead dwell in you, he that raised up Christ from the dead shall also quicken your mortal bodies by his Spirit that dwelleth in you."*

> *"Therefore, brethren, we are debtors, not to the flesh, to live after the flesh. For if ye live after the flesh, ye shall die: but if ye through the Spirit do mortify the deeds of the body, ye shall live. For as many as are led by the Spirit of God, they are the sons of God" (Romans 8:13-14).*

We cannot be double-minded when we think and say we will live for God. A lot of times people want to become Christians and follow Christ, but are not willing to totally give up the world. Test yourself. Do you have some of the following opinions?

"I want to do right but, although I am not married, I am not ready to give up pre-marital sex (fornication). How else can I keep a man/woman? Besides that, I like it! I can do everything but that."

"There's nothing wrong with going out to nightclubs as often as I want. I love to dance and I meet a lot of people (men/women) who are interesting."

Do these interesting people you meet have the same mindset as you (the mind of Christ)? Can you talk to them about your new life in Christ and they won't be bothered by your conversation? Will they encourage you to do things or say things that you have decided to let go?

"Well, I just won't talk about Jesus or God around them. I'll talk about what they talk about when I'm there. I'll talk about God when I'm around my Godly friends." Does this sound a little double-minded?

> According to James chapter 1:6-7, double-minded people should not think they will receive from the Lord. They are unstable in everything they do.

James says further in chapter 4:4, *"Ye adulterers and adulteresses, know ye not that the friendship of the world is enmity with God? Whosoever therefore will be a friend of the world is the enemy of God."*

It is also written in the Word of God (1 Corinthians 15:33-34 NIV), *"Do not be misled: 'Bad company corrupts good character.' Come back to your senses as you ought, and stop sinning; for there are some who are ignorant of God..."*

Be honest with yourself; evaluate whether you can afford to continue to live life as you have lived it until this point; or whether you need a change in your life that involves love, peace, joy, and power.

> Change is never easy, but very often, change is necessary.

The principles of the world are almost always in direct contrast to Kingdom principles. For example, the world says "get all you can and can all you get." In the

Kingdom, we learn that to give is more blessed than to receive (Acts 20:35). The world says "seeing is believing." In the Kingdom, we know that faith is the evidence of things unseen (Hebrews 11:1); Jesus says *"blessed are they that have not seen, and yet have believed"* (John 20: 29). The world encourages you to love those who love you. Jesus teaches His followers to *"Love your enemies, do good to them which hate you, bless them that curse you, and pray for them which despitefully use you"* (Luke 6:27). He says in Luke 6:32 (NIV), *"if you love those who love you, what credit is that to you?"* Your reward will be great if you love those who <u>don't</u> love you. You see, we have a very different mentality than the world.

If you choose to live for Christ, just relax; tell Him about all of your concerns, and surrender to Him. Put more emphasis on getting to know Christ than on trying to change yourself. You will find that as you discipline yourself to spend more quality time with Christ, as you learn more about Him and His Word, and as you press into His presence, you will not want to do the things you once did, and you will not miss them. Do not try to change yourself immediately; instead, get to know Christ intimately and allow Him to change you. When you meditate on His Word and pray for change, change will come. I believe you will not regret your decision to continue in the will of God. He will help you. In fact, He is the only one who can.

****

BEING REAL WITH YOURSELF AND OTHERS

One thing that you may find challenging when you decide to become a believer and disciple of Christ is sharing your testimony and faith with others. At times we tend to hide who we really are, and not share our real selves with others for fear of being ridiculed or rejected. No one wants to be ridiculed, and no one wants to be rejected. Being bold enough to say who you really are and what you really believe takes Spiritual maturity. It is a fact that you will lose some friends when you decide to come out of the world. Some people will not know how to deal with you when you say you are saved.

I remember once, before I was saved, that I liked a guy with whom I went to school. He and I hung out for a time and we went to nightclubs, etc. I really liked him, but we lost touch for a while. One day as I was cleaning out an old junk drawer, I ran across his number. I decided to give him a call because I thought maybe we could hang out again. I did reach him when I called. We had not chatted long before he told me he was saved. I almost choked. That meant he was now ... boring! He would not go out anymore, and he probably would try to get me saved...Nooooo! I wasn't ready for that. I was curious, though, to know why he made this decision.

He was a ladies' man and did not seem to be the type who would be saved. It was at this point that he shared his testimony with me. He didn't try to get me saved, he just told me of his experience. I was intrigued by his experience, but it was not enough to make me want to be saved at the time. I did, however, keep his words in my mind and could appreciate them and him more when I became saved.

Also, when you become saved, you will make mistakes in judgment as you mature. Sometimes you may say something that you really did not mean to say and offend someone. Or you may, on some occasion, be offended by something that someone else says. How do you handle the situation? Just be real with yourself first. When I say be real with yourself, I mean literally ask yourself how you really feel about the person, situation, what was said, etc. If he/she angered you, admit it to yourself. If you really feel like you hate this person, don't try to deny it. If you feel like you want to scream, scream (at the right time and place, of course). The point is to be open, tell yourself the truth, and don't feel like you have to hide the way you feel because you are a Christian. After all being a Christian has everything to do with the "Truth."

Once you are honest with yourself about the way you feel, go to God in prayer and tell Him all about it. Let Him know how the situation or the person made you feel and what you feel like doing about it. Ask Him questions and pray that He reveal His will to you in this situation. When you do this, be prepared to hear the answer. Sometimes, more often than not, you will have the mirror turned on you. God will often show you little things in your own personality or character that need to be changed.

You will hear from God if you are patient and sincere about receiving an answer. Your answer may be in His Word, or He may give you the answer through someone else you didn't even ask a question, or you may read it on a billboard, hear it in a sermon, or He may reveal it in a dream. God speaks in various ways if we are open and willing to receive Him.

Then, if it is appropriate, go to the person you offended or who offended you, and tell them the truth. Let them know how they offended you, or apologize for offending them. Your response should come after much prayer, and you should move as the Lord leads, and say only what you are led to say by the Spirit, not according to your flesh. A lot of situations need to be dealt with directly. Some situations require no response. It may be there to teach a lesson. Be led by God. Be real with yourself and others.

BEING TRUE TO YOUR CALL

Paul writes in Romans 1:16, *"I am not ashamed of the gospel of Christ: for it is the power of God unto salvation to everyone that believeth; to the Jew first, and also to the Greek."* Jesus says in Luke 9:26, *"For whosoever shall be ashamed of me and of my words, of him shall the Son of man be ashamed, when he shall come in his own glory, and in his Father's, and of the holy angels."* Would it not be a sad day if this statement is made about you or me when Jesus returns?

We, who profess to be followers and lovers of Christ, are sometimes ashamed of calling His name, telling others we are a Christian, saying "I am now saved," or of sharing our testimony with others. If we have concerns about talking about Christ, or sharing our faith with others, we should go back and continue our devotion time until we feel more comfortable sharing our salvation experience. We should again be real with ourselves and determine if we are really serious about the call. I know that it is hard sometimes bringing up the subject with friends or acquaintances who have not yet chosen Christ as their savior, but you have to know who you are in Christ and be strong in your beliefs and convictions about Him.

> This is not to say that you have to be overly aggressive and beat others over the head with the salvation message. It simply means that when the opportunity presents itself to say what you believe, you do not clam up and refuse to reveal who you are and what you believe.

God will reveal to you the gifts that He has already placed in you for the edification of the Kingdom. As Paul says to Timothy in 2 Timothy 1:6-14 (NIV), *"...fan into flame the gift of God which is in you... Do not be ashamed to testify about our Lord or ashamed of me His prisoner. But join with me in suffering for the gospel, by the power of God, who has saved us and called us to a holy life—not because of anything we have done, but because of His own purpose and grace... I am not ashamed, because I know whom I have believed and am convinced that he is able to guard what I have entrusted to Him for that day...Guard the good deposit that was entrusted to you—guard it with the help of the Holy Spirit who lives in us."*

You have been called to a holy life and are now a part of the Fellowship of Faith (the Fellowship of Believers; Body of Christ). Be true to your call. Guard the good deposit of faith that is in you, and be not ashamed of the gospel of Jesus Christ.

REVIEW

> ALMOST THERE

1. Do you remember your salvation experience? Discuss some trials and triumphs.

2. Define flesh and a self-centered life:

3. How does the natural man relate to a selfish/flesh life?

4. Are there any opinions that you have/had that are considered worldly? Explain:

5. What are your new thoughts on the subject?

6. Do we belong to Christ if we do not have His Spirit? Explain

7. List a few examples of how we should present Christ to others:

CHAPTER 3

SETTING UP A BASIC PROGRAM FOR PERSONAL STUDY

Your personal study and devotion time is very important to your spiritual growth. The more time you spend in devotion and study, the more you will be exercising your spiritual muscles and becoming greater in the Kingdom of God. You will be able to intelligently — moreover, spiritually — discuss and divide the Word of Truth. You will understand more and more about Jesus Christ and His gospel. Your knowledge, wisdom, and faith will increase as a result.

Make a commitment to pray and study the Word of God daily. This is your devotion or quality time with the Lord. This is the only way change comes in your spiritual life. It is amazing how you grow and change without even realizing it on a conscious level. The change is gradual and you will begin to notice that you are more spiritually grounded and centered in the Lord. You will find peace and confidence in the Word and in Jesus Christ. The Holy Spirit will help you as you endeavor to learn more about your walk with Christ.

> Be patient with yourself as you learn and know that some things will not be clear immediately, but you will understand them better as you continue to seek insight and understanding.

You will grow from one spiritual level to the next. It is similar to going to school or growing in this life by experience. You start out at a very low level. We can say at the beginning that you are in kindergarten or that you are a baby Christian. You will grow, as you continue to study and use the Word of God, into a "seasoned saint" rightly dividing the Word and using spiritual discernment to make good, sound decisions in your life.

Everyone grows at a different pace. What may be clear to one person may not be clear to the next. Again, be patient with yourself and pray for understanding and insight. How fast you learn depends on how much time you spend studying. You must put the time in study in order to get the most out of it. Hebrews 11:6 states *"But without faith it is impossible to please him: for he that cometh to God must believe that he is, and that He is a rewarder of them that **diligently seek Him**."* So be diligent in your search for the things of God and you will be rewarded.

There are basic materials that you need for Bible study and devotion. Some materials and books you should try to obtain are:

1. The Holy Bible – more than one version may be helpful
2. A concordance – this book (or on-line site) will help you find passages in the Bible
3. A Bible dictionary – this book (or on-line site) explains Bible words for clarity. A regular dictionary for looking up ordinary words will be helpful too.
4. Bible commentaries – these are helpful in explaining certain Bible passages for better understanding
5. A journal – this book will facilitate your learning as you use it to write down your experiences and feelings about certain things. It is a place where you can be honest with yourself about your attitudes and emotions. You may also track your progress during your spiritual growth.

The very best time to devote to study and meditation is early in the morning before anyone starts to stir inside or outside your household. Seek the Lord early when your time is not interrupted with the common activities of life. If possible, get up around 4:00 in the morning. This is a good time for quiet, peaceful prayer and meditation. You will have uninterrupted study time. If it is not possible for you to wake up and study at this time, plan a time when you are able to have uninterrupted study. As you mature in the Spirit, you will learn the value of early study.

> Plan the amount of time you will spend beforehand and try to stick to at least that amount of time. Start slow and then increase your study time.

Also, try to set aside a special place to study and use the same space each time. Do not use a place that is too comfortable, such as a bed or recliner. Sit up straight so that you will not be tempted to go to sleep.

Be aware that the devil, your enemy, does not want you to start this routine. He will bring all kinds of devices to deter your study. You will become aware of his devices and be able to avoid them eventually. One of his devices is to interrupt or disturb you any way he can. He will try to distract you and divert your attention elsewhere.

The phone will ring all of a sudden when it has never rung at 4:00 in the morning, someone in your household will awaken to ask you a question, the dog will bark, or you will all of a sudden become very sleepy. These types of things are bound to happen. Just be aware that they come to distract you, and be all the more determined to complete your study.

<u>It is important to pray often during your years of growth</u>. Try to pray at least three times per day, especially in the beginning when the devil, your flesh, and other forces are against you studying the Word of God. Pray for strength to do what is necessary to learn His precepts, commands, and will. Pray for understanding and perseverance, pray for covering and protection as you endeavor to get closer to the Lord. Pray for wisdom and understanding on how to apply what you have learned.

It is also important to note that there is a difference between reading the Holy Bible and studying the Holy Bible. Simply reading over chapters in the Holy Bible will not allow you to retain what you have read. Read a few chapters and then go back, study and meditate on what you have read. Commit certain verses to memory. Learn the stories in the Bible and the main personalities in the story. Get a chronological understanding of the events of the Bible. Spend extra time on a special study, some concept, or word you do not understand. Do a word search in a biblical internet site or search the concordance.

> Use whatever resources will help you in your study, being patient with yourself and the Holy Spirit as He reveals spiritual truths and gives you discernment.

****

DEFINITIONS

There are certain words and concepts in the Bible that you will need to understand from the beginning. The following terms and concepts will get you started on the right track:

Taken from the "MG Easton Illustrated Bible Dictionary"

- Christian – The name given by the Greeks or Romans to the followers of Jesus. It was first used at Antioch. The names by which the disciples were known among themselves were "brethren," "the faithful," "elect," "saints," "believers." But

as distinguishing them from the multitude without, the name "Christian" came into use, and was universally accepted.
- Salvation – Deliverance generally from evil or danger. In the New Testament it is specially used with reference to the great deliverance from the guilt and the pollution of sin wrought out by Jesus Christ "the great salvation" (Hebrews 2:3).
- Prayer –Converse with God; the intercourse of the soul with God, not in contemplation or meditation, but in direct address to him. Prayer may be oral or mental, occasional or constant. It is a "beseeching the Lord " (Ex 32:11)
- Trinity –A word not found in Scripture, but used to express the doctrine of the unity of God as subsisting in three distinct Persons. The propositions involved in the doctrine are these:

   1. That God is one, and that there is but one God (Deut 6:4; 1 Kings 8:60; Isaiah 44:6; Mk 12:29; Mk 12:32; John 10:30).
   2. That the Father is a distinct divine Person, distinct from the Son and the Holy Spirit.
   3. That Jesus Christ was truly God, and yet was a Person distinct from the Father and the Holy Spirit.
   4. That the Holy Spirit is also a distinct divine Person.

- Tithe – A tenth
- Born Again (Regeneration) – This word literally means a "new birth." In Titus 3:5 it denotes that change of heart elsewhere spoken of as a passing from death to life (1 John 3:14); becoming a new creature in Christ Jesus (2 Cor. 5:17); being born again (John 3:5); a renewal of the mind (Rom. 12:2).
- Tongues – Language; the words of Luke (Acts 2:9) clearly show that the various peoples in Jerusalem at the time of Pentecost did really hear themselves addressed in their own special language with which they were naturally acquainted.
- Kingdom of God – [God's] Christ's authority, or his rule on the earth; the blessings and advantages of all kinds that flow from this rule; the subjects of this kingdom taken collectively, or the Church.

- Eschatology – "A division of systematic theology dealing with the doctrine of last things such as death, resurrection, the second coming of Christ, the end of the age, divine judgment, and the future state." – (The Zondervan Pictorial Bible Dictionary 258)

****

STUDYING THE DIMENSIONS OF GOD'S WORD

God's Word, or the Holy Bible, is unlike any writing you have ever read before. If we think about it for a moment, the Holy Bible is a book that is still around and being diligently studied after thousands of years. The words have not changed; they may have been interpreted differently by different people or groups, but the core meaning remains the same. It is the only book known that I know of that people say you can read through in a "year." What book takes a year to read? It is a history book that has been tried, tested and proven to be accurate by some of the greatest historians and researchers. It has within its pages mysteries, examples, and truths that can change any life if practiced. It has been taught year after year after year in churches and schools all across the world. It is the only book that I know of that is the basis for <u>college</u> instruction (Bible Colleges).

The Holy Bible is the most scrutinized book of all time; it has the most third party evidence to support its claims than any other book in history. That is why I am so intrigued by it, and I am sure that you will be too.

The word *dimension* means aspect, component, facet, or phase. When I say that God's Word has many dimensions, I am saying that it has many components or facets. There is the written Word, or the words written on the pages of the Bible; and there is the "rhemah" or "logos" Word, the revealed Word of God spoken to your spirit. When you study and meditate on the Word, God often reveals to you its meaning or a truth to edify your spirit. With His "still small voice", God spoke to Elijah when he was running from Jezebel in 1 Kings 19:11-13. This voice speaks into your spirit also. He warns you of things that you need to be aware of, and advises you on what you are to do in a given situation; He is your helper.

****

UNDERSTANDING COMMANDS, STATUTES, DECREES AND PRECEPTS

When you understand the many facets of God's Word, you realize that in some situations, God gives us His <u>commands</u>. These commands are not negotiable. It is what God requires, there are no ifs, ands, or buts about it. It is what God says, it is what He means, and we can give Him no arguments about it. The Ten Commandments are an example of what God requires. They are not negotiable. When God says, "Thou shall have no other god before me," He will not allow another god. When a person decides to live for God, then **He is God** and there shall be no other god. If someone decides to worship an idol, he is breaking God's command.

A <u>statute</u> is a law or regulation that God puts in place to establish some type of ordinance or order, a permanent rule to govern the affairs of His people. An example of a statute put in place by God is in Numbers 27:8-11 (emphasis mine):

> *"And thou shalt speak unto the children of Israel, saying, if a man die, and have no son, then ye shall cause his inheritance to pass unto his daughter. And if he have no daughter, then ye shall give his inheritance unto his brethren. And if he have no brethren, then ye shall give his inheritance unto his father's brethren. And if his father have no brethren, then ye shall give his inheritance unto his kinsman that is next to him of his family, and he shall possess it: and it shall be unto the children of Israel a **statute** of judgment, as the LORD commanded Moses."*

A <u>decree</u> is a ruling or declaration of what God says will happen or a decision He firmly establishes. He decrees a thing, and it comes to pass; He decides a thing, and it is established forever.

David said in Psalms 2:7 (emphasis mine):

"I will proclaim the <u>decree</u> of the LORD: He said to me, 'You are my Son; today I have become your Father'."

A <u>precept</u> is a law or guideline for living. It is established as a result of an action. It is an "if," "then" concept (e.g. if you do this, then that will happen. If/when this is done, then that is established. If/when this happens, then that happens). It is the principle established because of an action. When the Pharisees asked Jesus if it was lawful for a man to put away his wife as Moses wrote, Jesus answered and said unto them, *"For the hardness of your heart he wrote you this <u>precept</u>"* (Mark 10:5, emphasis mine).

Moses' precept was as follows (Deuteronomy 24:1, emphasis mine):

> "**When** a man hath taken a wife, and married her, and it come to pass that she find no favour in his eyes, because he hath found some uncleanness in her: **then** let him write her a bill of divorcement, and give it in her hand, and send her out of his house."

Romans 10:9 has an important precept that is dependent upon a person's action. The precept that is established here is as follows (emphasis mine):

> "***If*** *thou shalt confess with thy mouth the Lord Jesus, and shalt believe in thine heart that God hath raised him from the dead, [**then**] thou shalt be saved."*

Jesus taught in Matthew 6:14-15 (emphasis mine), "***if*** *ye forgive men their trespasses, [**then**] your heavenly Father will also forgive you. But **if** ye forgive not men their trespasses, [**then**] neither will your Father forgive your trespasses."*

Understanding these concepts helps us to better understand the Bible and how to apply its truths to our lives. We will be blessed according to Psalms 1:1-3:

> *"Blessed is the man that walketh not in the counsel of the ungodly, nor standeth in the way of sinners, nor sitteth in the seat of the scornful. But his delight is in the law of the LORD; and in his law doth he meditate day and night. And he shall be like a tree planted by the rivers of water, that bringeth forth his fruit in his season; his leaf also shall not wither; and whatsoever he doeth shall prosper."*

The laws we now have are in our minds and in our hearts rather than in a written code of the old covenant (Hebrews 8:8b-10; Romans 2:13-16).

Please read over Psalms 119 to see examples of how commands, decrees, statutes, and precepts are expressed in the Holy Bible.

****

UNDERSTANDING HOW TO EFFECTIVELY STUDY AND USE THE HOLY BIBLE

The Holy Bible is an awesome book and not easily understood. It takes months and sometimes years to grasp a portion of its true meaning. As mentioned previously, simply reading the Bible is different from studying the Bible. It is important to study and learn the various commands, statutes, decrees, and precepts because these truths are the basis of our life decisions and standards.

There are many instructional booklets and online sites that teach you how to "read the Bible through in a year." In this lesson, I recommend a slightly different approach to studying the Holy Bible. I suggest obtaining a good Bible outline. Some Bibles contain an introduction and outline of each book of the Bible. The New International Version of the Bible has an excellent introduction and outline of book contents. Read through the chapter intros and outlines for the entire Bible. Become familiar with how it is organized and presented. Realize that there are many other books written by many people who witnessed the events of old testament times as well as Jesus' life. Not all books written made it into what is called the Christian "Canon of Scripture" or the books considered by Jews and early Christians to be divinely inspired by God and, therefore, accepted as scripture. There is an Old Testament canon and a New Testament canon. Together they are the 66 books of the Holy Bible, and have been studied and accepted for hundreds of years.

> The word *testament* means covenant or agreement that is contractual. The Holy Bible contains two testaments, the Old and New testaments. The Old Testament contains 39 books and the New, 27 books.

These books include:

THE OLD TESTAMENT

1) The Pentateuch – First five books of the Bible believed to be written, with the exception of the last part of Deuteronomy, by Moses.
2) The Old Testament History – Joshua through Esther
3) The Books of Poetry – Job through Song of Solomon
4) The Major Prophets – Isaiah through Daniel
5) The Minor Prophets – Hosea through Malachi

THE NEW TESTAMENT

1) New Testament History – Matthew through Acts
2) Paul's Epistles (letters) - Romans through Philemon
3) General Epistles – Hebrews through Jude
4) The Book of Prophecy - Revelation

The Standards of Christian Conduct

Certain information in the Bible, I believe, should be learned and quoted by any Christian <u>on demand</u>. This information includes the 66 books of the Holy Bible, the Ten Commandments, the Twelve Tribes of Israel, what makes up the Northern and Southern kingdoms of Israel, and Jesus' 12 apostles.

The 66 books of the Holy Bible are as follows:

The Old Testament

Genesis	II Chronicles	Daniel
Exodus	Ezra	Hosea
Leviticus	Nehemiah	Joel
Numbers	Esther	Amos
Deuteronomy	Job	Obadiah
Joshua	Psalms	Jonah
Judges	Proverbs	Micah
Ruth	Ecclesiastes	Nahum
I Samuel	Song of Solomon (Songs)	Habakkuk
II Samuel	Isaiah	Zephaniah
I Kings	Jeremiah	Haggai
II Kings	Lamentations	Zechariah
I Chronicles	Ezekiel	Malachi

The New Testament

Matthew	I Timothy
Mark	II Timothy
Luke	Titus
John	Philemon
Acts	Hebrews
Romans	James
I Corinthians	I Peter
II Corinthians	II Peter
Galatians	I John

The Standards of Christian Conduct

Ephesians
Philippians
Colossians
I Thessalonians
II Thessalonians

II John
III John
Jude
Revelation

The Ten Commandments (Exodus 20:1-17)

I   Thou shalt have no other gods before me
II   Thou shalt not make unto thee any graven image
III   Thou shalt not take the name of the Lord thy God in vain
IV   Remember the Sabbath day to keep it holy
V   Honor thy father and thy mother that thy days may be long upon the land which the Lord thy God has given thee.
VI   Thou shalt not kill
VII   Thou shalt not commit adultery
VIII Thou shalt not steal
IX   Thou shalt not bear false witness against thy neighbor
X   Thou shalt not covet

The Twelve Tribes of Israel (Genesis 35:23-26)

(Note: Israel is the name given by God to Jacob, Isaac's son as stated in Genesis 32:27-28 and Genesis 35:9-13. The twelve tribes are named after Israel's sons)

Reuben
Simeon
Levi
Judah
Issachar
Zebulun

Gad
Asher
Dan
Naphtali
Joseph
Benjamin

The Northern and Southern Kingdoms (I Kings 11-12 NIV)

All of Israel was one kingdom and was ruled first by King Saul, then King David, then King Solomon. After Solomon became king, he married many foreign women — Moabites, Ammonites, Edomites, Sidonians, and Hittites. They were from nations about which the Lord had told the Israelites, "You must not intermarry with them, because they will surely turn your hearts after their gods." Nevertheless, Solomon held fast to them and his wives turned his heart after other gods. So Solomon did evil in the eyes of the Lord. He did not follow the Lord completely. Although the Lord had forbidden Solomon to follow other gods, Solomon did not keep the Lord's command.

Since Solomon did not keep the Lord's covenant and decrees, the Lord tore the kingdom away from Solomon and gave it to one of his subordinates. The Lord did not do it during Solomon's lifetime for the sake of his father David, but tore it out of the hands of his son. He did not tear the whole kingdom, but gave him one tribe for the sake of David, and for the sake of Jerusalem. Ten tribes were taken from King Rehoboam, Solomon's son, and given to Jeroboam, his servant. The towns of Judah (and Benjamin) remained loyal to Rehoboam. The northern kingdom (ruled by Jeroboam) became known as Israel, and the southern kingdom (ruled by Rehoboam) became known as Judah.

Jesus' Twelve Apostles (Matthew 10:2-4)

Peter	Thaddaeus (Judas, son of James?)
Andrew	Thomas
James	Matthew (Levi)
John	Simon the Zealot
Philip	James, son of Alpheus
Bartholomew	Judas Iscariot (who betrayed Him)

****

There are also Bible timelines that will help you understand when certain events and points in history happened. You will become familiar with the acronyms B.C. (Before Christ) and A.D. (*anno domini* or "in the year of our Lord." Some say "After Death," but it is thought to be an erroneous definition).

After becoming familiar with the outline of the Holy Bible and committing the above information to memory, begin to read the entire Bible. Some people begin reading in the New Testament, then the Old Testament. The New Testament, being written originally in Greek, is easier for some to understand, while the Old Testament, written in Hebrew, is closer to the original text for others. The choice is yours.

Some say the Old Testament is prophecy of what is to come. The New Testament is the prophecy fulfilled. Both speak of the coming Christ or Messiah. The Messiah comes in the New Testament. He lives, dies, and is raised again to life to fulfill prophecies spoken about Him in the Old Testament. He was with God in the beginning and He returned to God after His resurrection.

> In reading and endeavoring to understand the Holy Bible, we understand better God's divine plan of salvation, which is both for now and is ultimately eschatological in its fulfillment.

When you begin to read the Holy Bible, you will want to learn some passages and quote them at a later time when needed in certain situations. There may be difficult times when you need to be reminded of what God has said through one of His prophets or through His Son. One scripture that I like to quote a lot is one from Philippians 4:6-7 (NKJV) which says *"Be anxious for nothing, but in everything by prayer and supplication, with thanksgiving, let your request be made known to God; and the peace of God which surpasses all understanding, will guard your hearts and minds through Christ Jesus."*

Earlier, it was suggested that a Bible concordance be obtained to help find passages in the Bible. This book will prove invaluable when you're trying to find certain verses in the Bible and you can only remember a word or few words. Looking up the word you remember will lead you to the scripture; book and verse. Most Bibles have a concordance located in the back. This is very useful when you need to find a passage quickly. The Strong's Exhaustive Concordance is a very good tool to have because it has thousands of Bible passages that you can look up by word. It is not a book, however, that is small and can be carried everywhere. It is rather large and is good to use in your personal Bible study at home. There are also Bible concordances online that are good to use if you have access to a computer.

We should become so familiar with the Holy Bible and Bible stories that when a pastor begins to preach from certain passages, we are able to recognize the story and the book from which it is taken almost immediately. And when the pastor says to turn to, for example, Hosea 3:10, we should not fumble through the Bible or turn to the table of contents on a regular basis. We should know the books of the Holy Bible so that we will know where to go when a scripture is mentioned. Many times the scripture is already read and the pastor is on to something else by the time we look the book up in the table of contents and find the page on which it is located.

> There is nothing wrong with making use of the table of contents until you become familiar with the books of the Bible, but it will be better for you once the books are committed to memory.

Remember in your study of the Holy Bible that it will take time to learn what you need to learn, and the Holy Spirit will help us learn it if we diligently seek Him. It may take some longer than others to master naming the 66 books of the Bible, The Ten commandments, or the Twelve Tribes of Israel; but be patient with yourself and persevere. You will gain more knowledge as you **study** God's Word.

****

RIGHTLY DIVIDING THE WORD OF TRUTH

II Timothy 2:15 states, *"Study to show thyself approved unto God, a workman that needeth not to be ashamed, rightly dividing the word of truth."*

The first word in this passage of scripture indicates that it is not enough to simply read the Word, but it is necessary to study it. Once we study the Word of God, we will be more equipped to discuss it. Things that are <u>studied</u> are well known by the one studying it. He is very familiar with it and is prepared to discuss it without wavering.

Suppose you studied extensively for a school test on "The Preamble to the Constitution." You are familiar with the words and can recite the preamble if called upon to do so. Further, you know when the preamble was written and who wrote it. You know about the time period in which it was written. You can explain why it was written and the impact it has on the citizens of the United States. There is nothing about the preamble to the Constitution that you cannot speak about. In fact, if you hear someone say something about the preamble that is not correct, you immediately recognize the error and can probably refer that person to the resource that can prove your point in the disagreement so there will be no need for too much debate.

The Preamble to the Constitution reads as follows:

"We the people of the United States, in order to form a more perfect union, establish justice, insure domestic tranquility, provide for the common defense, promote the general welfare, and secure the blessings of liberty to ourselves and our posterity, do ordain and establish this Constitution for the United States of America."

The Standards of Christian Conduct

If someone began to quote the preamble by saying:

"Four score and seven years ago our fathers brought forth, upon this continent, a new nation, conceived in liberty, and dedicated to the proposition that all men are created equal…,"

a person knowing the preamble to the constitution would immediately know that this is an incorrect quote for the preamble. This quote begins the Gettysburg Address, not the Preamble to the Constitution.

In the same way, if someone knew the Holy Bible or at least part of it well, they would be able to tell if it was misquoted. If someone knew Jesus Christ, they would be able to tell if someone else said something about Him that was incorrect. For example, if someone said "Jesus Christ was born in New York City," most people who even heard about Christ would know that the statement was absurd. New York City was not even built in Jesus' day.

If someone said "Jesus Christ was born in Nazareth in Galilee," this statement might throw some people and some may believe it. Nazareth was a town in Galilee and Jesus spent much of His time there; He even lived there for awhile. It takes someone who really knows Jesus through Bible study, to know that Jesus was born in Bethlehem in Judea. This is stated in Matthew 2:1 and Luke 2:4-7. If someone asked you where Jesus was born, you could say with confidence, if you looked up the scripture, that Jesus was born in Bethlehem in Judea. If you read a little more, you would know that Joseph and Mary lived in Nazareth in Galilee and went to Bethlehem in Judea to register for the census as ordered by Caesar Augustus. While there, Mary (Jesus' mother) gave birth to Him. So although Joseph and Mary lived in Nazareth in Galilee, they were in Bethlehem in Judea at the time of Jesus' birth. A lot of people thought that Jesus was born in Nazareth because that's where his parents lived. If a person studied scripture, they would not be ashamed because they did not know where Jesus was born. In explaining how He came to be born in Bethlehem, instead of Nazareth, they would have rightly divided (explained) the Word of Truth.

> This is how Jesus would like for us all to be — a workman that doesn't need to be ashamed, rightly explaining the "Word of Truth." In order to be that workman, we have to **study** to show ourselves approved unto God.

Please read handout #5 and take the Jesus trivia challenge. How did you do?

UNDERSTANDING THE IMPORTANCE OF PRAYER AND MEDITATION

We have previously established that prayer is communion with God. We communicate with God through our prayers. We exalt, adore, worship, thank, and petition God in our prayers. We also intercede for others, confess our sins, ask for forgiveness and submit to God in our prayers. Prayer is done corporately (in an assembly of people) and privately (in our own home or space). It is recited together with others or done individually. However or whenever it is done, it is our way of linking up our spirit with His Spirit. It is very important for us as believers and very important to God as our Father.

> I Thessalonians 5:17-18 states *"Pray without ceasing. In everything give thanks: for this is the will of God in Christ Jesus concerning you."*

What would you do if you could not talk with your earthly father or mother? This is the case for some people. Even if the relationship is strained, there is always a void in one's life if their ability to have a good relationship with their parents was taken away. It is the same with our Heavenly Father. In order to have a good relationship with Him, we must communicate with Him. We must listen to Him and obey Him because He knows what is right for us. We can let Him know how we feel about things and ask Him for help in our lives and our decisions. The Lord speaks to us in a still small voice. It is more of an impression we experience when He gives us a word of encouragement or warning.

I cannot stress enough how important it is to spend quality time with the Father; to listen to Him and be guided by His Holy Spirit. Believe it or not, the Lord does speak to us. We just have to understand how to hear Him. When we set aside our special time with Him — preferably in the mornings before anyone has a chance to stir — it is a time of learning, a time of listening, a time of confessing, a time of prayer, and a time of worship and praise. All of these elements come into play when it is done sincerely and consistently.

The Lord has so much to reveal to us, but our lives are so busy and filled with things to do that we miss what He is saying to us. The Lord is speaking to us all the time; we are just not able to hear Him when our minds are filled with the worries of the day or other distractions.

Distractions are bound to come, but when they do, be all the more determined to overcome these distractions. Say to the devil, "The Blood of Jesus is against you." Pray for the Blood of Jesus to cover you as you devote time to study and pray that the Lord will hold back the hands of the enemy.

<u>Always pray before you begin your study</u>. Thank Him for your daily bread (the Word), and ask God to open your mind and your heart to hear what thus says the Lord. Many times when we begin to pray, our minds may become distracted also. You may find yourself thinking, during prayer, about what's ahead in the day or about something that happened in the past few days or hours. When this happens, you are not communicating with God, but trying to recite a rote prayer out of habit. Stop your recital and begin to talk to God as if He was sitting beside you. When you hold a conversation with God, you are concentrating on Him and His goodness and His awesome power. It is a good idea to begin by reverencing Him, then thank Him for your blessing, then confess with your mouth the sins you may have committed, ask for forgiveness, pray for others in need, supplicate for the saints and ask for what you need. Pray for insight and understanding of His Word. **Note: read Proverbs Chapter 2.**

Jesus' disciples asked Him to "teach us to pray" in Luke 11:1-4. Let's read the account of this teaching:

"And it came to pass, that, as he was praying in a certain place, when he ceased, one of his disciples said unto him, Lord, teach us to pray, as John also taught his disciples."

"And he said unto them, 'When ye pray, say,

"Our Father which art in heaven, Hallowed be thy name. Thy kingdom come. Thy will be done, as in heaven, so in earth. Give us day by day our daily bread. And forgive us our sins; for we also forgive every one that is indebted to us. And lead us not into temptation; but deliver us from evil.'"

This prayer became popularly known as "The Lord's Prayer." A slightly different account is in Matthew 6:5-14.

After prayer and praise, open your Bible and begin to read. Be prayerful about where to start. Some people like to start at the beginning and read to the end. Some say the New Testament is a good place to start. Others say the Gospel of John is a good place to start. However you begin, be prayerful about it. Meditate on the words you read. <u>Pause and think about what you read, repeat silently, or mutter His Word</u>. Read the passage again and ask questions about it. Read the cross references given in the passages. Take notes on what you are reading and research other scriptures on the subject.

The Lord will eventually reveal truths to you. When this happens, try to write down what was revealed. You will not remember it later, so it helps to write it down when it is first revealed. Keep a pad and pen near your bed because many times truths are revealed to us in dreams or thoughts while we are in a relaxed state. Write down what you hear for future reference.

Sometimes when God has revealed a thing to me, I may think it is for someone else. I am full of zeal for God's Word and I am eager to share it. Usually the word for someone else is an admonition (a mild rebuke). I have learned however, especially in early stages of growth, that revelation from God is usually for the hearer and not for someone else.

> Do not be too quick to tell someone, "God told me to tell you..." without first checking to see if it is for yourself. He may be telling you something you think is for someone else.

How awesome is revelation from God! It hits you like a ton of bricks and it is something that you know could not have come from you. It is profound and usually has you feeling endued with power. Persevere in studying and reading the Word of God. The more you study and meditate on it, the more you will be confident of what it says and will be able to rightly divide the Word of Truth.

It is evident in a person's life when they have spent quality time with God. You can tell because the words spoken by the person are sincere, honest, spoken with confidence and are the truth.

> Again, growth in the Spirit is evidenced by the time spent in prayer and meditation. It will come naturally even without your noticing it. You will find that you are more centered and the worries of life don't get you down as much.

You will find too, however, that you will be tested on the Word you study. Growth or promotion does not come without a test. You will be reminded of the Word you studied in your everyday life. God wants us to not only be hearers of the Word, but doers also. Old habits will be tested and pruned from your life. <u>Welcome the training and the discipline from the Lord</u>. Realize it is for our own good and for our growth.

Never neglect your devotion time. This is where we get the Heavenly game plan from God, so we can live on earth as it is in Heaven. It is most vital to this Christian life. Without it we will find ourselves straying and being entangled again in the world's affairs. We must never trade eternal Spiritual truths for temporal or worldly views. It is easy to do when we slack off on our prayer and meditation time. Even if it does happen, begin again to devote quality time to prayer, study and meditation. It is the most valuable tool in our Spiritual growth.

****

REVIEW

SETTING UP A BASIC PROGRAM FOR PERSONAL STUDY

1. Define Eschatology
   _____

2. What is meant by a statute?
   _____

3. What day/time have you committed to meet with God in Bible study and devotion?
   _____

4. How many books make up the Christian "Canon of Scripture"? _____

5. List as many books of the Old Testament you can remember:
   _____
   _____
   _____

6. List as many books of the New Testament as you can remember:
   _____
   _____
   _____

7. Can you name the 12 Tribes of Israel?
   _____
   _____
   _____

8. List Jesus' 12 Apostles:
   _____
   _____

9. Discuss how prayer and meditation have affected your life:
   _____
   _____

CHAPTER 4

RELIGION vs. RELATIONSHIP

A negative connotation has sometimes been attached to the word *religion*. It is often referred to as a rigorous set of rules and traditions that has nothing to do with a relationship. It is religiously carrying out a practice or tradition in an often mechanical way. The Holy Bible says in James 1:26-27(NIV), *"If anyone considers himself religious and yet does not keep a tight reign on his tongue, he deceives himself and his religion is worthless. Religion that God our Father accepts as pure and faultless is this: to look after orphans and widows in their distress and to keep oneself from being polluted by the world."*

> Religion in its proper context is good, but taken out of context it is a perversion of what is true and righteous.

God speaks of the obstinacies of His people in Isaiah 29:13 when He says, *"Wherefore the Lord said, Forasmuch as this people draw near me with their mouth, and with their lips do honor me, but have removed their heart far from me, and their fear toward me is taught by the precept of men."* Our idea of religion and God's religious plan are very different in many ways.

My true Christian experience began when I was about 29 years old. Although I was brought up in the church and knew about Jesus Christ, I did not begin a personal **relationship** with Him until I had already been considered a Christian. I was a regular member of the church, a member of the choir, and even sang in a family group visiting from church to church. I did mechanically what I was told (and what I thought) was the right thing to do. I must admit, during these times of regular church going, I really did not understand what it was all about. I did what everyone else was doing. Sometimes it seemed right and sometimes I questioned what was really going on. I did not understand everything I saw in the church environment because some practices seemed contrary to what I read in the Holy Bible. Sometimes I did things that seemed so natural and accepted in the world, but I knew it was contrary to what I read in the Holy Bible.

However, I always had a longing within me to know more; to get the true knowledge of what Christianity was all about. I was given a book about the Bible that intrigued me as it talked about Jesus Christ and the miracles He performed while on earth. It had Bible stories in it that were fascinating to me. I read more because something was missing in my religious experience.

****

THE MOST IMPORTANT RELATIONSHIP

I came to know Jesus personally as stated earlier around age 29. I was hospitalized for gall bladder surgery. I had to have a blood transfusion during that time and prayed, "Lord let this be your blood flowing inside of me." I had people praying for me, including my mother, who is a prayer warrior, and certain preachers. After surgery, I had an experience which I will never forget. One night I lay in bed with an oxygen mask attached to me. All of a sudden, I was unable to breathe. My mother, who was in the room with me, immediately called for the nurse, then began to pray. Whatever they did to me at the time relieved my breathing difficulty and I was able to fall asleep. The next morning when I awoke, it appeared as if a dark cloud was moving away from my eyes. Since then, I felt a presence that would talk to me and answer questions in one way or another that I had about Spiritual things. I believe that the presence was the person of Jesus Christ. I wasn't well versed in the Bible, but I began reading it from that point.

This experience began my determination to learn more about Jesus. There had to be something to this "Christ-centered life." I became saved and have been on a journey and quest for knowledge ever since. I cannot say that I was consistent in my walk at first, but I was always drawn back to the righteous path. It has not been easy, but I can say that I have found peace and contentment.

I heard a sermon that changed the way I communed and spent time with the Lord. It spoke about spending devotional time with Him, and praying 3 times per day. When I began to do that, a whole new revelation of Him opened up to me, and when I heard these revelations, I would write them down. I would also write things that I studied, and that I had heard in a sermon or teaching I thought was significant. <u>These experiences led me to what I call a true relationship with Christ</u>. I understood better what the Christian experience should be about and I liked and accepted the truth that was revealed to me by Jesus Christ Himself either through God's Word, His servants, or through His Spirit. I came to understand the most important relationship; that is the relationship between me and the eternal God through Jesus Christ, His Son.

****

KNOWING GOD FOR YOURSELF

It is very easy to look at people, church, and preachers and make judgments about how bad they are or how hypocritical they are. It is true that there are a lot of false preachers and a lot of false teachings going on in the world, just as the Bible says there would be. 2 Peter 2:1-3 states, *"But there were false prophets also among the people, even as there shall be false teachers among you, who privily shall bring in damnable heresies, even denying the Lord that bought them, and bring upon themselves swift destruction. And many shall follow their pernicious ways; by reason of whom the way of truth shall be evil spoken of. And through covetousness shall they with feigned words make merchandise of you: whose judgment now of a long time lingereth not, and their damnation slumbereth not."* The Lord Himself will deal with false teachers and preachers.

What is not easy to do is judge ourselves to see if we are not counted among the hypocrites. Do we do what the false prophets, preachers, teachers, and Christians are doing? If so, are we not as bad as they? Some say, "I know that I am not right and I don't want to be a hypocrite, so I will just stay in the same condition I am in. At least I do not pretend to be a saint. I am being real!" Now that would be a true statement except I believe those that make such statements are not truly being real with themselves. I believe that they are just as torn as anyone else about doing the right things, and they long to know the truth of Christ and Christianity. I believe they call on the name of God and Jesus when they are in trouble. I believe they know in their heart of hearts that He is real.

> Because there are so many hypocrites in the church, Christianity has gotten a bad reputation. It does not make it any less true, pure, and right. The true meaning, like many other things in life, has been perverted by the world and by enemies of Christ.

It is very important, therefore, to get to know God and Christ, His son, for yourself. You cannot make decisions about Him and Christianity based on what you see and hear. In order to make a right judgment, you must find out for yourself who He is and whether a relationship with Him is worth pursuing. Regardless of what people say or what you think about Christianity, you cannot make a right judgment unless you have tried it for yourself.

Try to know Jesus for yourself. I do not believe you will be disappointed once you get to know Him and His power. You will know a peace which cannot be taken away from you by the world. As you know Him more and more, a faith in Him and His ways will be developed. You will then know that you can trust Him to lead, guide, and protect you. It is up to you. You will never know the benefits of knowing and following Jesus until you try Him. Even if you do not choose to live a life with Christ, at least you would be able to speak about Him from your own experience and know what you are talking about instead of listening to what others say.

There is also the issue of whether the Lord God is the only true God or whether Christianity is the only true religion. With so many religions in the world, like Buddhism, Islam, or some new wave religion, it may be hard to know which is right. I have heard some pose the question, "How do we know that Christianity is the way to go? Other people believe strongly that their religion is right. How do we know that they are not right and Christians are wrong?" To these individuals I say, "If you feel strongly that one of them is right for you, choose that religion." See if following Buddha or Mohammed is best. You should not choose any religion, however, until you have deeply researched it. I don't know about any other religion because I have not personally tried any other.

I myself had questions about Christianity when I looked at how others who were called Christians conducted themselves, and when I heard a message from a Christian preacher that just did not sound right. <u>It was only when I researched for myself, and experienced the Spirit of God, that I was convinced that Christianity was right for me.</u> Again, you have to choose whom you will serve, but make a choice. As for me, I will serve God. I decided to make Jesus my choice.

You may ask, "Do you choose Jesus as your Lord or God?" Well, Jesus is the Son of God; He was sent to this earth to die for our sins; He lived, died, and rose again with all power in His hands; He was given all authority in heaven and on earth (Matthew 28:18). He says in John 10:30, "I and my Father are one." To truly choose the one and only living God is to choose Jesus Christ because no one comes to God the Father without going through Christ Jesus (John 14:6). Likewise, no one comes to Jesus Christ unless the Father draws him (John 6:44). There is nothing like knowing someone first hand. You can hear about a person from someone else and that will give you some idea of how that person is or his/her personality. But you are given information based on someone else's perception. We know that one person's perception may not be the same as another's. It is best to know the person for yourself.

Has the Bible's True Meaning been Lost in Translation?

The question as to whether the Holy Bible is true has come up. Has some of its true meaning been lost in translation? What about the Apocrypha or the Dead Sea scrolls? These are questions you will have answered as you study for yourself. Pray and ask God to reveal His true Word to you. Personally, I believe some other manuscripts are true. My basic rule is I choose to believe in the Holy Bible as written. I believe other manuscripts or teachings as long as they agree with the Holy Bible. It is true that certain original meanings may have been diminished in translations, but the original meaning can be researched in earlier translations or in the Hebrew or Aramaic language.

I also believe what Peter says in 2 Peter 1:20, *"Knowing this first that no prophecy of the scripture is of any private interpretation. For the prophecy came not in old time by the will of man: but holy men of God spake as they were moved by the Holy Ghost."*

The Holy Bible is still on the best sellers list even after thousands of years. That in itself says something to me about how powerful it is. Jesus says in Matthew 24:35, *"Heaven and earth shall pass away, but my Words shall not pass away."*

****

THE CRY FOR KNOWLEDGE AND WISDOM

How is it that we get to know someone or some information? Is it not true that we must spend time with that person or study that information? The same is true in getting to know the Lord. Usually when we start out as Christians, we have a general knowledge of who God is and who His Son is. Many of us were made to go to church or Sunday school and we heard the Bible stories and the strong sermons on the omnipotent God. Now we must move beyond what we have heard and get to know Him for ourselves. It does not matter who God was to Momma or Daddy or to Reverend *so and so*. What matters now is finding out for yourself who God is to you and who His Son is to you.

The Holy Bible says in Revelations 3:20, *"Behold, I stand at the door, and knock: if any man hear my voice, and open the door, I will come in to him, and will sup with him, and he with me."* The Lord extends an invitation for us to get to know Him. The best way to do this is to pray to Him and study Him in His Word. You will find a wealth of information that no one could have explained sufficiently to make you understand how deep and wide is His love for us. We must learn to spend "quality" time with the Father. That means setting aside a special time that is just for you and Him. He has some special messages that are just for you and would like to share things with you that are just between you and Him.

Since He made you, He would like to show you who you are in Him, and show you some things about yourself which are not a part of what He created you to be. If you are willing, then He can make you over to be all that He intended for you to be. He will share His love, power, wisdom, righteousness, and peace with you. As you get to know Him better, you will be changed to be like His Son, who has all power and authority in the heavens and on earth. You will escape the corruption in this world and participate in the promise He has in store for those who love Him and are obedient to His Word.

Proverbs 2:1-6 says, "*My son [or daughter], if thou wilt receive my words, and hide my commandments with thee; So that thou incline thine ear unto wisdom, and apply thine heart to understanding; Yea, if thou criest after knowledge, and liftest up thy voice for understanding; If thou seekest her as silver, and searchest for her as for hid treasures;* **Then** *shalt thou understand the fear of the LORD, and find the knowledge of God. For the LORD giveth wisdom: out of his mouth cometh knowledge and understanding,*" (emphasis mine).

> If you persevere in Him, and allow Him to teach you, you will understand what is right and just and fair and receive a rich welcome into His Kingdom prepared for those who **endure**.

Life in Christ

Life in Christ does not mean freedom from grief and trials. These are necessary for our growth as we begin to be pruned from our old ways and habits. Life in Christ does mean, however, guidance through the trials and peace in the midst of a storm.

This peace increases as our faith in God increases; as we understand that God does have everything under control even though we may not understand His methods, nor have our desires manifested in the way we expect them. We must relinquish what we know for what He knows, and who we are for who He is. This is a lifelong journey and we will not understand everything in this lifetime. Be assured, however, that you will understand a lot more than you did before you decided to make your life His life. The issues of this life become clearer to you as you learn of Him and trust His way. You will finally realize that His way is right, just, and fair and that a lot of our worries or concerns are groundless (this is wisdom).

Many have endeavored to explain the meaning of life using horoscopes, tarot cards, psychics, etc. You will notice that when someone writes a book on the discovery of self, or how to find happiness in the world, they always come back to biblical principles, sometimes without even realizing it. They use phrases such as "getting in touch with your inner self or power" and "finding yourself." They do not realize or maybe do not acknowledge that this inner power is the Holy Spirit within us. He is someone greater than self; He is the power within us that can move us beyond difficulties and circumstances that we cannot control.

> When we allow the power within us to control our lives instead of trying to control it ourselves, we find wisdom, knowledge, and peace. This power is the power of the Holy Spirit.

****

IN ALL YOUR GETTING...

It is stated in Proverbs 4:7, *"Wisdom is the principal thing; therefore, get wisdom: and with all thy getting get understanding."* In the NIV Bible, it is stated a little differently. It says, *"Wisdom is supreme, therefore get wisdom. Though it cost you all you have, get understanding,"* (emphasis mine). Here we see that wisdom (knowledge of what is true and right coupled with good judgment) and understanding (perceiving the meaning of; grasping the significance or importance of) are very important in our Christian walk.

Read what the Holy Bible has to say about understanding, instruction, and knowledge (all emphases mine):

Proverbs 1:7 - *"The fear of the LORD is the beginning of knowledge: but fools despise wisdom and instruction."*

Proverbs 3:5 - *"Trust in the LORD with all thine heart; and lean not unto thine own understanding."*

Proverbs 17:27 - *"He that hath knowledge spareth his words: and a man of understanding is of an excellent spirit."*

Proverbs 18:2 - *"A fool hath no delight in understanding, but that his heart may discover itself."*

Proverbs 19:8 – *"He that getteth wisdom loveth his own soul: he that keepeth <u>understanding</u> shall find good."*

Proverbs 19:20 - *"Hear counsel, and receive <u>instruction</u>, that thou mayest be wise in thy latter end."*

THE SPIRITUAL

A Spiritual understanding of things and happenings is far superior to our temporal (pertaining to temporary worldly things) understanding. To understand the importance of the Spirit, let us read what the Holy Bible says about the Spirit (emphases mine):

Zechariah 4:6 – *"Then he answered and spake unto me, saying, this is the word of the LORD unto Zerubbabel, saying, not by might, nor by power, but by my **Spirit**, saith the LORD of hosts."*

John 4:24- *"God is a **Spirit**: and they that worship him must worship him in **spirit** and in truth."*

Romans 8:4-5 - *"For they that are after the flesh do mind the things of the flesh; but they that are after the **Spirit** the things of the **Spirit**. For to be carnally minded is death; but to be **spiritually minded** is life and peace."*

Romans 8:26-27 - *"The **Spirit** also helpeth our infirmities: for we know not what we should pray for as we ought: but the **Spirit** itself maketh intercession for us with groanings which cannot be uttered. And he that searcheth the hearts knoweth what is the mind of the **Spirit**, because he maketh intercession for the saints according to the will of God."*

Luke 11:13 – *"If ye then, being evil, know how to give good gifts unto your children: how much more shall your heavenly Father give the **Holy Spirit** to them that ask him?"*

Luke 12:11-12 – *"And when they bring you unto the synagogues, and unto magistrates, and powers, take ye no thought how or what thing ye shall answer, or what ye shall say: For the **Holy Ghost** shall teach you in the same hour what ye ought to say."*

John 3:5-6 - *"Jesus answered, verily, verily, I say unto thee, except a man be born of water and of the **Spirit**, he cannot enter into the kingdom of God. That which is born of the flesh is flesh; and that which is born of the **Spirit** is **spirit**."*

In order to grasp or understand Spiritual truths, one would have to disconnect from all that is of the physical senses (sight, hearing, smell, taste, touch) and allow things of the heavenly unseen to enter into his being (holiness, righteousness, truth, love, peace, wisdom and joy). How do we move into this state?

The following is one formula for connecting with the Holy Spirit:
(See also the section on being real with yourself and others in Chapter 2)

1. Be still before the Father and quiet your mind of thoughts pertaining to this world.

2. Breathe slowly and deeply for a few moments. Release any tension and stress you may be experiencing and continue to breathe and relax.

3. Pray a simple prayer to the Father that may go something like this:

   Father in heaven, your name is hallowed in all the earth. Your kingdom come and your will be done in this earth and in me as it is in heaven. Father I thank you for keeping me as I sojourn on this earth.
   Thank you for providing for me and not allowing me to be utterly cast down. Thank you for moving obstacles seen and unseen out of my path. Thank you for your Holy Spirit that leads, guides, and directs me daily.
   I invite your presence into my being now. I open my heart so that you may come in and sup with me. I confess that I have sinned against you and your Spirit (confess any sin that you may have committed) and I ask for your forgiveness as I forgive others their sins against me. According to your word, I am anxious for nothing. I come to you Father with these petitions… and I cast my cares upon you for I know you care for me. These and other blessings I ask in Jesus' name. Amen.

4. Allow your mind to focus on whatever things are true, lovely, just, pure, and of good report in your life or someone else's life. Praise God for these things and thank Him for whatever is good in your life or the lives of others.

5. Focus your attention on the Holy Spirit and allow Him to be absorbed into your being.

6. Continue to relax your mind and body for as long as is needed.

Try to practice this getting away and meditating on God and good daily.

Jesus says in Matthew 13:15, *"For this people's heart is waxed gross, and their ears are dull of hearing, and their eyes they have closed; lest at any time they should see with their eyes, and hear with their ears, and should understand with their heart, and should be converted, and I should heal them."*

When we do not apply ourselves to understanding Spiritual things and concepts, we harden our hearts to the Spirit. We sometimes take offense to things we do not understand. We also rebel against what we do not understand. That is why the Bible says in all your getting, get understanding.

In Romans 12:2 it states, *"And be not conformed to this world: but be ye transformed by the renewing of your mind, that ye may prove what is that good, and acceptable, and perfect, will of God."*

Please read handout # 6 on "Understanding the Mind" in chapter 11

****

THE SEARCH FOR TRUTH

I cannot say enough about how important "truth" is in our Christian experience. We have already explored scriptures dealing with truth. Jesus said in John 8:31-32 to the Jews who believed Him, *"If ye continue in my word, then are ye my disciples indeed; and ye shall know the truth, and the truth shall make you free."*

There is freedom in not only knowing the truth, but exercising truth in all you do and say. The worldly saying "honesty is the best policy" was probably taken from a biblical truth. It is, nonetheless, a good policy to keep. Be honest, not only with yourself, but with all you come in contact with. Sometimes, truth hurts; but a lie hurts worse.

In this Christian experience, we sometimes come in contact with false teachers and false preachers of "the Word" or the Holy Bible. They come in sheep's clothing, but are actually ravenous wolves. They speak eloquently and tell of things that may make sense in a worldly way, but have no Spiritual basis. They cause the unsuspecting person who is not well versed in the Word themselves to stumble and fall away from the truth.

This is why it is so important to search out the truth for ourselves. The Holy Bible says in Matthew 23:8-10, *"But be not ye called Rabbi: for one is your Master, even Christ; and all ye are brethren. And call no man your father upon the earth: for one is your Father, which is in heaven. Neither be ye called masters: for one is your Master, even Christ."* This means that Jesus Christ is our one Master and any person that comes before us should be teaching what Jesus taught.

Be very leery of teaching that does not line up with the Word. It is very important to know the scriptures for ourselves. This way, we will be able to "rightly divide the Word of Truth" as mentioned in II Timothy 2:15.

Test Religious Words against Scripture

Be very careful when reading religious books or information other than the Holy Bible, and test whether the book or information agrees with the Holy Bible. There are many wonderful books about Christianity, God, and religion that give us insight into the Word and further explain scripture; or they give us practical knowledge about the Bible and how to live a Christian life. We should read and listen all we can to good, Bible-based instruction for our lives.

If you ever hear or read something that does not quite sound right to you or does not quite line up with scripture, or you have a question about what was heard or read, always write it down and go back to the Holy Bible to research the issue for yourself. Ask trusted teachers of the Word about the issue for clarification on where it is in the Holy Bible and read it for yourself. Above all, pray to God for clarification of something you do not understand.

A good, well-meaning preacher or teacher may slip sometimes and say something that is not in the Bible, but taught among fellow ministers, etc. Always research the issue for yourself. If it is appropriate (be prayerful about it), go back to the one who said the thing that was confusing and ask for a reference or — if you have researched it and found what they said to be untrue or incomplete — let them know your reference so they can research it and possibly make a correction. You must, however, be prayerful about addressing the issue. If the Lord does not lead you to talk to the person, DON'T DO IT!

There are many versions of the Holy Bible and many manuscripts about biblical truths giving all kinds of information. There are also all kinds of biblical scholars and teachers of the Bible. As long as the teaching lines up with the Word and you feel comfortable that it is truth, listen attentively. If it does not line up with the Word, cast down what you heard and do not receive it. I have found the New International Version (NIV), New King James Version (NKJV) and King James Version (KJV) of the Holy Bible to be very helpful. I cross reference them for ease of understanding.

The Holy Bible says in 1 John 4:1-6, *"Beloved, believe not every spirit, but try the spirits whether they are of God: because many false prophets are gone out into the world. Hereby know ye the Spirit of God: Every spirit that confesseth that Jesus Christ is come in the flesh is of God: And every spirit that confesseth not that Jesus Christ is come in the flesh is not of God: and this is that spirit of antichrist, whereof ye have heard that it should come; and even now already is it in the world.*

Ye are of God, little children, and have overcome them: because greater is he that is in you, than he that is in the world. They are of the world: therefore speak they of the world, and the world heareth them. We are of God: he that knoweth God heareth us; he that is not of God heareth not us. Hereby know we the spirit of truth, and the spirit of error."

> As we grow in the things of the Spirit, we will understand better how to test spirits to see if they really are from God. Anyone who says they know the true and living God should also know Jesus Christ, His Son.

****

The Standards of Christian Conduct

REVIEW

> RELIGION vs. RELATIONSHIP

1. What relationship, in which you are currently involved, is most important to you and why?

2. On who or what do you base your opinion of Christianity? Explain

3. What is the best way to get to know God?

4. Does life in Christ mean freedom from grief and trials? Yes___ No ___

5. If we have faith in Jesus, what are we assured of through our grief and trials?

6. What does it the word "temporal" mean?

7. What does it mean to be Spiritual?

8. What does it mean when the Bible says, "For these people's heart has become calloused…"?

9. What are ways that we can prevent our hearts from becoming calloused?

10. Why is it important to know the Holy Bible for yourself?

CHAPTER 5

Understanding Christian Standards and Principles

There are certain standards and principles you will find in the character of a Christian. These standards and principles are what we live by. These are the traits that separate a Christian from a non-Christian. People recognize us as Christians whether we tell them or not by how we carry ourselves and by the Spirit that is operable in us. It is very apparent, especially to other Christians but also to worldly people. The difference is that Christians can appreciate the Spirit in other Christians, but worldly people cannot totally understand us and, therefore, some cannot appreciate who we are and what we stand for. Because they don't understand us, they may criticize the way we present ourselves and what we say. They will rebel against our ways and sometimes reject us altogether. This is to be expected among people in the world. Do not be surprised at the criticism, rejection, and misunderstanding of the world. The Bible says we are a peculiar people and this is true because Christ is not known to a lot of them. They may have heard about Christ, but do not really know Him or accept Him into their lives.

The most important standard that a Christian lives by is the requirement (that is commandment) to love. Love for God first, then love for our neighbors. Jesus says in Mathew 22:37-40, *"Thou shalt love the Lord thy God with all thy heart, and with all thy soul, and with all thy mind. This is the first and great commandment. And the second is like unto it, Thou shalt love thy neighbour as thyself. On these two commandments hang all the law and the prophets."*

God is love. Therefore, every principle is based in love.

To love someone is to consider their needs, feelings, and well being. It does not mean to provide for others' needs only and neglect our own, but to provide for their needs as we provide for our own; to treat people as we would like to be treated; to love them as we love ourselves. Jesus also says in Matthew 7:12, *"Therefore all things whatsoever ye would that men should do to you, do ye even so to them: for this is the law and the prophets."*

To love people means to see people as Christ sees them in the Spiritual, not as we see them in the natural. You never know when or if Christ might call that person that we consider a heathen to a great service, and that heathen in our eyes will repent and become greater in the Kingdom than we believe we are. That is also why the Holy Bible says, "Do not judge." You never know how God is working in the lives of others in ways that we do not see or understand.

Many "love" verses in the Bible can be found in 1 Corinthians 13:1-13, Matthew 5:43-46, John 13:34-35, Romans 12:9, Romans 13:8, 1 Peter 1:22, 1 Peter 2:17.

The Holy Bible says in James 1:19 (NIV), *"My dear brothers, take note of this: Everyone should be quick to listen, slow to speak and slow to become angry."* Everyone is not at the same stage of growth. It is no use trying to convince a sinner to be saved when he has no interest. Instead, what will draw him is your life by example, not words. Also, if you have something exciting to share, don't be too eager to share it with someone who is sharing their excitement with you. First, hear them out, be excited for them, share in their happiness; then, if it is appropriate, share your story. Know that you are not the only person that God is using, and do not feel you have to counsel all the time. God is using many people. Sometimes He's sending a word for you. Listen, be quiet and listen!

Let these come from your lips: encouragement, praise, fairness, approval, acceptance, love. Live with these: tolerance, fairness, security, friendship, and love. The results are these: patience, confidence, appreciation, justice, faith, and love.

****

LOVE

Let's look a little further into the concept of love. It is the basic principle and virtue necessary for the Christian religion. We are known by our ability to love and love has to be sincere (Romans 12:9).

Love is the greatest commandment. All the law and the prophets are fulfilled in keeping the commandment of love (Mathew 22:40; Romans 13:10). Love God first, and then love your neighbor as yourself. Because love is a commandment, there is no room for negotiation. When God gives a command, it is settled.

We **must** learn and discipline ourselves to love. It may not come naturally, but it can be accomplished in a spiritual way. Pray for more love to be poured into your heart and pray for understanding of the God-kind of love that is unconditional. When we learn to treat people as we would like to be treated, instead of how they treat us, then it becomes easier to love. Loving this way is not conditional on how one treats us, but how we would like to be treated.

Thus:

The way we treat people = the way we would like to be treated

Not

The way we treat people = the way people treat us

The other person's actions or words are taken out of the equation.

It is stated in Luke 6:31-33 (NIV), *"Do to others as you would have them do to you. If you love those who love you, what credit is that to you? Even sinners love those who love them. And if you do good to those who are good to you, what credit is that to you? Even sinners do that."*
Colossians 4:6 states *"Let your speech be always with grace, seasoned with salt, that ye may know how ye ought to answer every man."*

> Be cheerful when speaking to others, sincere when there is an issue, and always honest and truthful. Be sincere and honest about your feelings to yourself first, then to God, then to others. Confess when you have done wrong. Try to right the wrong, if possible.

Most people come from a less than perfect background. We came from homes that were not functioning properly; in fact, most of our homes were dysfunctional. Either we grew up in a home where there was no mother figure present or no father figure; or if mother and father were there, the relationship lacked love and truth.

Many of us have been abused in some form in our lives, usually beginning in our own homes whether it was physical abuse, verbal abuse, emotional abuse, or mental abuse through manipulation. It becomes a difficult undertaking to overcome the affects of abuse (anger, pain, bitterness, loneliness, depression, rage, low self image, promiscuity, law breaking, carelessness, rigidity in thinking, competitive spirit - trying to prove you are worthy, rebellion, and difficulty giving **and** receiving love).

We behave the way we do based on the environment from which we came, whether it be our homes or communities. The character we have, or lack of it, comes from the experiences we had growing up. Even if we did not come from the ideal home where there was plenty of love, acceptance and appreciation, <u>there is still hope for us in Christ Jesus</u>. Because God is love, we have a right to tap into the love of God — that unconditional, pure, sincere, unselfish kind of love. Through Jesus Christ, we learn to accept and respect the power of God's love. We are able through His blood to be released from our past and become new creations in Christ. 2 Corinthians 5:17 says, *"Therefore if any man be in Christ, he is a new creature: old things are passed away; behold, all things are become new."*

It is hard to convince ourselves that we are worthy of such a deep and abiding love, especially if we have never experienced true love. It may be hard to accept at first, but time and application of the love principles will enable us to experience love like we have never experienced it before. We must love **first** as Christ loved us first, and we must love people even with all their faults as Christ loved us even with all our faults. This is a hard concept to understand and accept, but through perseverance and asking God for understanding and grace, we can obtain it, perform it, and experience it in great measure!

We must renew our minds about love, life, and people. We must begin to see ourselves and people in a new way. Romans 8:38-39 states, *"For I am persuaded, that neither death, nor life, nor angels, nor principalities, nor powers, nor things present, nor things to come, nor height, nor depth, nor any other creature, shall be able to separate us from the love of God, which is in Christ Jesus our Lord."*

> Just as nothing can separate us from the love of God, nothing should be able to separate people from our love. This will be a slow, gradual, and seemingly impossible task, but with God all things are possible. We **will** overcome in the "LOVE" area, and love is how we will overcome in all areas of our lives.

If we are unable to understand and **receive** God's love, we will never be able to give it. It is hard to believe, but we will actually reject the love of God if we do not understand it and accept it; just as we would reject His will for our lives when we don't understand it. We don't understand that though we don't see it yet, it is the very best thing for us.

The biggest block to receiving love, especially the abundant love of God, is "self." We don't even understand how or when this happens, but if we are not open to the love of God because the flow is blocked by self, it is averted to other channels. We miss out on His love and healing power because we were not open to accept it. Our minds are too focused on what we need, what we have, how we are hurting, how we are so furious with someone, what we have to do, where we need to go, <u>self pity</u>, and on and on and on. We have not quieted our minds and human spirits to connect with God's Holy Spirit. We have not spent that quality time with God for healing and love.

Begin by penciling quality time with God into your busy schedule. It should be first priority on your schedule, but if you have not grown to that level yet, just pencil Him in when you can. Go to a quiet place and have an honest talk with the Lord about yourself, your day, feelings you still have about your father, mother, your past, etc. Confess everything that is in your heart; all those feelings of anger and pain, loneliness and fear. For me, writing it down is therapeutic; for others, just stating what is in their hearts is sufficient. Then allow God to enter into your space and heart. Relax and release the pressure, pain, anger and hurt. Allow the love of God to be absorbed into your being; meditate on the love of God by reciting verses from the Holy Bible dealing with love. Some examples are (emphases mine):

<u>Psalm 103:1-5</u> - *Bless the LORD, O my soul: and all that is within me, bless his holy name. Bless the LORD, O my soul, and forget not all his benefits: Who forgiveth all thine iniquities; who healeth all thy diseases; Who redeemeth thy life from destruction; who crowneth thee with <u>lovingkindness</u> and tender mercies; Who satisfieth thy mouth with good things; so that thy youth is renewed like the eagle's.*

<u>Psalms 59:16</u> - *But I will sing of your strength, in the morning I will sing of your <u>love</u>; for you are my fortress, my refuge in times of trouble.*

<u>John 3:16,</u> - *"For God so <u>loved</u> the world that he gave his one and only Son, that whoever believes in him shall not perish but have eternal life."*

<u>John 15:13</u> – *"Greater <u>love</u> has no one than this: to lay down one's life for one's friends."*

<u>Romans 8:28</u> – *"And we know that in all things God works for the good of those who <u>love</u> him, who have been called according to his purpose.*

<u>Romans 8:35, 37-39</u> – *"Who shall separate us from the <u>love</u> of Christ? Shall trouble or hardship or persecution or famine or nakedness or danger or sword? No, in all these things we are more than conquerors through him who <u>loved</u> us. Neither height nor depth, nor anything else in all creation, will be able to separate us from the <u>love</u> of God that is in Christ Jesus our Lord."*

Psalm 23 (NKJV): - *"The Lord is my shepherd; I shall not want. He makes me to lie down in green pastures; He leads me beside the still waters. He restores my soul; He leads me in the paths of righteousness for His name's sake. Yea, though I walk through the valley of the shadow of death, I will fear no evil; for You are with me; Your rod and Your staff, they comfort me. You prepare a table before me in the presence of my enemies; You anoint my head with oil; my cup runs over. Surely goodness and mercy shall follow me all the days of my life; and I will dwell in the house of the Lord Forever."*

Romans 12:9 (NIV) – *"<u>Love</u> must be sincere. Hate what is evil; cling to what is good"*

Say out loud, "My love for God and others is sincere. I hate what is evil; I cling to what is good."

Romans 13:8 (NKJV) – *"Owe no one anything except to <u>love</u> one another, for he who loves another has fulfilled the law."*

Say aloud, "I owe no one anything except love."
Meditate on what love is in order to understand it and accept it; meditate on 1 Corinthians chapter 13:1-8 often:

> *Though I speak with the tongues of men and of angels, and have not charity [love], I am become as sounding brass, or a tinkling cymbal. And though I have the gift of prophecy, and understand all mysteries, and all knowledge; and though I have all faith, so that I could remove mountains, and have not charity [love], I am nothing. And though I bestow all my goods to feed the poor, and though I give my body to be burned, and have not charity [love], it profiteth me nothing. Charity suffereth long, and is kind; charity envieth not; charity vaunteth not itself, is not puffed up, Doth not behave itself unseemly, seeketh not her own, is not easily provoked, thinketh no evil; Rejoiceth not in iniquity, but rejoiceth in the truth; Beareth all things, believeth all things, hopeth all things, endureth all things. Charity never faileth.*

It is very important to understand the above verses of scripture. To me it means: though I am very smart and have a lot of degrees and Grammy Awards, I always give to the poor, I always pray for the sick, I took my children <u>and</u> their friends to the circus, I made an "A" on my paper, I tithe faithfully, and I believe for my healing etc.; if I do not **have** love, I am nothing and it was all for nothing.

If I **have** love, then I am patient and kind, I am not jealous, I am not proud, I do not behave badly, I am not easily angered, I am happy with truth, I always persevere, I always hope, always believe, and I never fail to love.

> In order to **give** love, we must first **have** love. If we have love, then we have God because God is love.

Do something good for someone each day; whether it is a kind word, deed, prayer, or helping out in some small way. You may not be received as expected with some people, but do not stop. This exercise is for your benefit as well as theirs. It may feel awkward at first, but make it a practice and see how kindness flows back to you.

Try to erase or cast down critical, cynical, and mean thoughts about yourself or other people. Yes, certain people are mean, unfair, and downright evil and may not deserve kindness. Just remember not to allow yourself to be one of those people. It is their problem if they are not willing to release anger or evil from their lives. Your change begins on the inside of you, so you must do what is necessary to allow Jesus to change your heart. Keep praying and reading your Bible and asking God to pour His perfect love into your heart that casts out all fear. Strive to recognize the presence of the Lord in each moment of your day and acknowledge His presence. Thank Him during the day and speak to Him during your day. Ask Him to lead, guide, and direct your path. Ask that He keep the enemy away from you during the day and if anyone comes to you, let them be from Him. Ask that He guide your tongue and if any words come from your mouth, let them be His words and not your own from a carnal and fleshly mind.

> Learn to smile more and <u>choose</u> to be happy and cheerful. God works best in a cheerful heart. Do not be afraid ... the Lord is with you. He will keep you and sustain you throughout the day.

While at work, pray that God gives you the grace to work as if you are working for Him, and not for man, because your reward will come from Him, and not from man (Col 3:23). Do your best at whatever it is you do. Try not to grumble and complain. If you do, ask for forgiveness and thank God for employment.

> At home, be as loving as you can toward your family members. Say something nice to your spouse if married and/or your children. Give a compliment each day. Try to make a habit of it.

If you have had a rough day, let your family member(s) know, and ask to have a few moments alone to rest and pray. Acknowledge your anger or pain, and be truthful with yourself about your feelings and situations that occurred. Forgive any hurt that you have been a victim of so that God will forgive you when you trespass against Him.

Put God first in your heart, your soul and mind as someone to treasure and adore. To love God with all your heart, soul, and mind is to cherish Him with all your conscious intentions; to bring Him to mind and embrace every thought of Him, to purposefully treasure Him in your memory, opinions, thoughts, and intellect; to pay loving attention to Him; to bring Him to mind in an endearing way; to care about and obey Him willfully.

To love your neighbor is to have a strong affection for your fellow man. It means to have mercy on him/her and look out for his/her well-being. Love must be sincere (Romans 12:9); therefore, practice love daily. You will reap the rewards if you do not faint. <u>Give love and it shall be given to you</u>, pressed down, shaken together and running over.

> Make deposits regularly into your love bank. You will be able to make a large withdrawal when needed or when desired. **Learn to love and laugh daily**. Again, it will be hard at first, but you will reap its benefits if you persevere in it!

****

FORGIVENESS

Everyone knows that our God is a forgiving God, but what most don't say is that if we do not forgive, we will not be forgiven (Matthew 6:14-15). It is imperative, therefore, that we learn how to forgive others so that our heavenly Father will forgive us.

When someone offends us, mistreats us, or wrongs us in some way, it is a natural reaction to be angered, embittered, hurt, or given to retaliation. In the kingdom of God, however, we are to allow God to repay others for the wrongs they have done to us.

Romans 12:17-21 states, *"Recompense [repay] to no man evil for evil. Provide things honest in the sight of all men. If it be possible, as much as lieth in you [depends on you], live peaceably with all men. Dearly beloved, avenge not yourselves, but rather give place unto wrath: for it is written, Vengeance is mine; I will repay, saith the Lord. Therefore if thine enemy hunger, feed him; if he thirst, give him drink: for in so doing thou shalt heap coals of fire on his head. Be not overcome of evil, but overcome evil with good."*

This is a new concept for most because we have learned throughout our lives to treat others the way they treat us. To do unto others <u>before</u> they do unto you. Not so in the kingdom of God; our avenger is the Lord. We do not have to fight. The battle is not ours, it is the Lord's. So whenever someone does us wrong, it is our duty to take it to the Lord and let Him handle it. We are to express our emotions (like anger, resentments, rage, hurts, etc.) in the presence of God alone.

You would want to be totally honest with yourself first about what you are feeling. It is not uncommon for us Christians to pretend we feel a certain way about a situation or a person because we feel that Christians are not supposed to feel negatively toward that situation or person. But the truth is that we really dislike the person or situation. We cannot pretend we feel a certain way and say we love the person if it is not true. God knows our hearts and he knows when we are being hypocritical about what's in our hearts. Why not confess to yourself the way you really feel even if it is not a righteous feeling? It is not wise or honest to pretend.

> One good method of connecting to how you really feel about a situation or person is to write down what happened in a particular instance or situation and how that made you feel. Be very honest with yourself.

Write down the emotions you felt (anger, sadness, bitterness, joy, pain, etc). Also write down how what you said to someone might have made them feel. Continue to write until you have on paper every word, feeling, conversation, activity, action, and reaction involved in the situation. It is important not to think too hard about what was said or your feelings. Just let the pen write without thinking too much about what you are going to write. Afterwards, read what you have on paper. Evaluate the situation and what was said. Evaluate how you felt or how the other person might have felt. You will be surprised how this release can free you from what you have had on your chest. Next, ask yourself questions about how you handled the situation or person. What are some words you spoke that should not have been said? What did someone say to offend you? Assess how you could have better handled the situation. Did you say something to offend or hurt? Did someone offend or hurt you?

After you have gotten in touch with how you really feel about the situation or person and have been honest with yourself, now you can be honest with God. Confess to the Lord your fault in the situation. Also let Him know how the other person hurt you.

Pray to the Lord for forgiveness for how you handled the situation if it was not handled properly and in a Christian-like manner. Ask Him to take away the offense and hurt you may be feeling. Ask Him to give you wisdom in the way you act toward people, making the most of every opportunity. Ask Him to guide your tongue when speaking and "allow your conversation to be full of grace and sincere seasoned with salt, so that you will know how to answer everyone," (Colossians 4:6).

Now it may be time to make a call and get it right with the person you offended or who may have offended you. Ask for forgiveness for your part in the misunderstanding or disagreement. Tell the person what they did to offend you (speaking the truth in love) per Matthew 18:15-17. Be prayerful, however, about when or whether to contact the person and what to say. Always be led by the Spirit and have peace about what you do and say. If you have no peace, it may be wise to wait and continue talking to the Lord until that peace comes. There is a time and place for everything. Let everything be done decently and in order.

This is for our benefit more than for the benefit of the person who wronged us, because we would want the Lord to show mercy on us when we fall and mess up. In order for Him to do this, we must forgive men their faults. If we have unforgiving hearts, we are blocking the Spirit and blessings that the Lord has in store for us.

> Unforgiveness separates us from God and we are not able to hear when He speaks to us. We are always required to forgive; so if things are not going well for you and you are not able to connect with the Spirit, check your heart to see if there is any unforgiveness there.

Colossians 4:12-13 says, *"Put on therefore, as the elect of God, holy and beloved... mercies, kindness, humbleness of mind, meekness, longsuffering; Forbearing one another, and <u>forgiving one another</u>, if any man have a quarrel against any: <u>even as Christ forgave you, so also do ye</u>,"* (emphasis mine).

If you have unforgiveness in your heart, immediately repent, forgive and right the wrong if possible with whomever you have not forgiven. Do not allow unforgiveness to hinder your walk and block your communication with God or your blessings. Again, remember, forgiveness is mostly for your benefit.

UNDERSTANDING HUMILITY

When we hear the word "humble" or "humility", we sometimes associate it with the word "weak." Yet, to be humble is very far from being weak. Proverbs 25:28 states, *"He that hath no rule over his own spirit is like a city that is broken down, and without walls."* You are not prideful, but confident. You are not boastful, but meek. You use your power wisely, not foolishly. It takes a great man or woman to be humble. It takes sincerity and respect, and it must be genuine. If it is not, then it is called false humility and is easily recognized.

> When you are humble, you recognize that there is a power greater than you and you give honor and respect to this power.

For Christians, this power is God. When you learn to respect the power of God, you cannot help but be in awe of His very presence. You realize your limitations compared to His unlimited power. You recognize that He is great compared to your lowliness. You also recognize that whatever power or strength you have is because of Him.

Paul says in Colossians 3:12 (NIV, emphasis mine), *"Therefore, as God's chosen people, holy and dearly loved, clothe yourselves with compassion, kindness, **humility**, gentleness and patience.*

James states in James 3:13 (emphasis mine), *"Who is a wise man and endued with knowledge among you? let him shew out of a good conversation his works with **meekness** of wisdom."* <u>It takes wisdom to be humble.</u>

Peter states in 1 Peter 5:5 (emphasis mine), *"Likewise, ye younger, submit yourselves unto the elder. Yea, all of you be subject one to another, and be clothed with **humility**: for God resisteth the proud, and giveth grace to the **humble**."*

Christ showed His humility to man by washing His disciples' feet in John 13:3-5:

Jesus knowing that the Father had given all things into his hands, and that he was come from God, and went to God; He riseth from supper, and laid aside his garments; and took a towel, and girded himself. After that he poureth water into a bason, and began to wash the disciples' feet, and to wipe them with the towel wherewith he was girded.

He said in verses 14-17, *"If I then, your Lord and Master, have washed your feet; ye also ought to wash one another's feet. For I have given you an example, that ye should do as I have done to you. Verily, verily, I say unto you, the servant is not greater than his lord; neither he that is sent greater than he that sent him. If ye know these things, happy are ye if ye do them."*

Therefore, we are not self-righteous, but we realize that our righteousness comes from Him. We are not conceited or prideful, because we recognize that if it was not for His Holy Spirit moving in us, we would be nothing.

****

REPENTANCE

To repent means to not only regret your words or actions that are sinful, but to also change your words or actions because you understand that they were wrong and you want to please the Lord. This is a very important concept in establishing a new life with Christ. If we decide we want to turn from our former way of life and live for Christ, we must repent of our past sins, which means we recognize what those sins are, confess those sins, regret that we have committed those sins, turn from those sins, and change the way we think and conduct ourselves. We learn how to renew our minds according to scripture, and we accept God's standard of thinking and living. It is not just feeling sorry for what we have done; it is changing the way we think or act because we regret what we have done.

John the Baptist was a forerunner of Christ. Before Christ began His ministry, John baptized people in water for repentance. This act meant that the person baptized decided to die to his old way of life and be raised to the newness of life in Christ Jesus. They were baptized in (or into) the name of the Father, the Son, and the Holy Spirit. The act was done for the forgiveness of sins as stated in Mark 1:4 (NIV), *"And so John the Baptist appeared in the wilderness, preaching a baptism of repentance for the forgiveness of sins,"* and Luke 3:3, *"And he came into all the country about Jordan, preaching the baptism of repentance for the remission [forgiveness] of sins."*

When we repent of sins, we prove that repentance by our deeds. We no longer speak and act like a sinner, but we begin to speak and act like a person of Godly character and integrity. We show that we no longer wish to be the old person, but we are made new in our minds according to Romans 12:1-2, *"I beseech you therefore, brethren, by the mercies of God, that ye present your bodies a living sacrifice, holy, acceptable unto God, which is your reasonable service. And be not conformed to this world: but be ye transformed by the renewing of your mind, that ye may prove what is that good, and acceptable, and perfect, will of God."*

John admonished the people to also produce fruit in keeping with repentance in Luke 3:8. This is showing by your good deeds out of a Godly character that you have changed. Repentance is not just a suggestion by God; it is a <u>command</u>, just as love is a <u>command</u>.

Take a look at the following verses regarding repentance (emphases mine):

Acts 17:30 (NIV) – *"In the past God overlooked such ignorance, but now he commands all people everywhere to **repent**."*

Acts 26:20 – [Paul speaking] *"But shewed first unto them of Damascus, and at Jerusalem, and throughout all the coasts of Judaea, and then to the Gentiles, that they should **repent** and turn to God, **and do works meet for [demonstrating] repentance**."*

2 Corinthians 7:10- *For godly sorrow worketh [brings] **repentance** to salvation ... but the sorrow of the world worketh [brings] death.*

2 Corinthians 12:21 (NIV) - *I am afraid that when I come again my God will humble me before you, and I will be grieved over many who have sinned earlier and have not **repented** of the impurity, sexual sin, and debauchery in which they have indulged.*

2 Peter 3:9 (NIV) - *The Lord is not slow in keeping his promise, as some understand slowness. Instead he is patient with you, not wanting anyone to perish, but everyone to come to **repentance**.*

Revelation 2:20-22 – Jesus referring to the church at Thyatira – *"Notwithstanding I have a few things against thee, because thou sufferest [tolerated] that woman Jezebel, which calleth herself a prophetess, to teach and to seduce my servants to commit fornication, and to eat things sacrificed unto idols. And I gave her space to **repent** of her fornication; and she **repented** not."*

Revelation 9:20-21(NIV) – *"The rest of mankind who were not killed by these plagues still did not **repent** of the work of their hands; they did not stop worshiping demons, and idols of gold, silver, bronze, stone and wood—idols that cannot see or hear or walk. Nor did they **repent** of their murders, their magic arts, their sexual immorality or their thefts."*

What else can be said about the importance of repentance? It is necessary to be saved and enter into the Kingdom of Heaven. But God gives us grace and He will help us in our weaknesses if we are sincere and diligently seek His face. If we allow Him, He will change our hearts. Let it not be said too late. Accept Jesus Christ now and begin to live apart with Him and in Him.

****

DENYING SELF

Jesus said in Matthew 16:24, *"If any man will come after me, let him <u>deny himself</u>, and take up his cross, and follow me,"* (emphasis mine). In this statement, Jesus is expressing to us that we are His vessels; instruments for His use. He has a mighty and great commission for us, and we must be ready and equipped for service. He will make the opportunities and the plans. It is our duty to rid ourselves of all that hinders our progress. That is our cross. Usually it involves ridding ourselves of our selfish ways and allowing Jesus to use us for and in His plan. Believe me, He has a plan for our lives and for the lives of others who may not yet know Him or have accepted Him. If we are still holding on to fleshly desires and selfish ways, we are not ready for service. He was crucified on the cross for our sins. Now we have to take up our cross and have those fleshly and self-centered ways crucified on it. We have to die to greed, anger, resentments, selfish ambitions, jealousy, impurity, fornication, adultery, strife, etc.

> Once we have dealt with ourselves and conquered the weaknesses within ourselves with the help of the Holy Spirit, then we are better equipped for service in the Kingdom.

To deny self also means withholding things from ourselves that we may crave, such as food (for a period of fasting), entertainment (for a time of consecration), sex (when we know it is out of order), or sleep (when we need to spend quality time in devotion with God). This is a form of discipline in order to train ourselves for service in His kingdom.

We may have to retreat from a party that is getting out of hand with excessive drinking, inappropriate behavior or language because we know that it is not fitting for a man or woman of God. We may have to do something or go somewhere that we would prefer not go help someone in need or deliver a word to someone we would rather not talk to. All of this is denying self and obeying the voice of the Holy Spirit.

Romans 6:6-7 states *"Knowing this, that our old man is crucified with him, that the body of sin might be destroyed, that henceforth we should not serve sin. For he that is dead is freed from sin."*

Romans 6:11-14 states, *"Likewise reckon ye also yourselves to be dead indeed unto sin, but alive unto God through Jesus Christ our Lord. Let not sin therefore reign in your mortal body, that ye should obey it in the lusts thereof. Neither yield ye your members as instruments of unrighteousness unto sin: but yield yourselves unto God, as those that are alive from the dead, and your members as instruments of righteousness unto God. For sin shall not have dominion over you: for ye are not under the law, but under grace."*

Note: Refer to the Principle of Denying Self in Chapter 9

****

DEVELOPING A STRONG, NOBLE, CHRISTIAN CHARACTER

We hear this phrase often among Christians, "God is good all the time and all the time, God is good!" It is a true statement. God is also love, full of mercy, grace, and wisdom; He is a God of order and He is pure; He is a just God; He is not weak; He is strong and mighty!

Jesus Christ is the same as His Father. He says that He does what His Father does and says what His Father says (John 5:19; John 8:28). Jesus is the same yesterday, today, and forevermore. Jesus has a noble (of a high moral quality), majestic, glorious, courageous, and bold character; yet He is as meek as a lamb when it comes to obeying His Father's will.

What about you? Are you good all the time? Are you loving, full of grace, mercy and wisdom? Are you an orderly person? Is your heart pure? Are you just? Are you strong and mighty? Are you the same person (not double minded, hypocritical, or two faced) everyday? Do you have a noble character, personality, or reputation like Jesus has? If not (and many of us can say we do not have a character like Jesus Christ), do not worry. We can begin to develop a character like Christ's character so that we may be strong, mature, and complete, not lacking anything.

> If we are to be ambassadors of Christ, we need to conduct ourselves like He does. Just as Jesus does what His Father (our Father) does, we need to do what Jesus does.

Our minds need to be conformed to think like Jesus. Philippians 2:5 states *"Let this mind be in you which was also in Christ Jesus."* Know that this will not come immediately; it takes prayer, discipline, perseverance, and love for Christ.

Do not fret, and do not be dismayed! The Holy Bible is filled with every character building method we will need. This takes patience and a belief that we can do it. I don't care how bad, sad, ruthless, mean, tired, wicked or weak your personality was before Christ, it is going to change into one that is strong, powerful, good and pleasing in God's sight. In addition to the principles already mentioned, let's look at what the Holy Bible says about who we are in Christ, what our character should be, and what to do to change it.

Paul says in Ephesians 2:1-4:24 (NIV):

> *"As for you, you were dead in your transgressions and sins, in which you used to live when you followed the ways of this world and of the ruler of the kingdom of the air, the spirit who is now at work in those who are disobedient. All of us also lived among them at one time, gratifying the cravings of our sinful nature and following its desires and thoughts. Like the rest, we were by nature objects of wrath.*
>
> *But because of His great love for us, God who is rich in mercy, made us alive with Christ even when we were dead in our transgressions—it is by grace you have been saved. And God raised us up with Christ and seated us with Him in heavenly realms in Christ Jesus…For we are God's workmanship, created in Christ Jesus to do good works, which God prepared in advance for us to do…remember that formerly you who are Gentiles (not of Jewish decent) by birth…were separate from Christ, excluded from citizenship in Israel and foreigners to the covenants of the promise, without hope and without God in the world.*
>
> *But now in Christ Jesus you who once were far away have been brought near <u>through the blood of Christ</u>…Consequently, you are no longer foreigners and aliens, but fellow citizens with God's people and members of God's household…You were taught, with regard to your former way of life, to put off your old self, which is being corrupted by its deceitful desires; to be made new in the attitude of your minds; and to put on the new self, created to be like God in true righteousness and holiness."*

Peter says in 1 Peter 2: 9-10, *"But ye are a chosen generation, a royal priesthood, an holy nation, a peculiar people; that ye should shew forth [proclaim] the praises of him who hath called you out of darkness into his marvellous light, which in time past were not a people, but are now the people of God: which had not obtained mercy, but now have obtained mercy."*

What does a good, Godly character look like in these days and times? The same as it did back in Bible days. You basically hold fast to the principles that you learn in the Holy Bible, you treat people the way you would want to be treated, you stand strong in your beliefs and honor God.

Colossians 3:17 states, *"And whatsoever ye do in word or deed, do all in the name of the Lord Jesus, giving thanks to God and the Father by him."* Verse 23 also states, *"And whatsoever ye do, do it heartily, as to the Lord, and not unto men [as if working for the Lord and not for men]."* You understand that the source of whatever you need is God and you will receive a rich reward here on earth and in heaven if you do not faint and give up.

> Exhibit your royal, charismatic personality everywhere you go and in all you do. Be bold, yet peace-loving before the world, and humble before your Father in heaven.

From Ephesians 4:25 through the end of Ephesians, we are told what to do to purify our characters and to put on the whole armor of God. Let's look at some characteristics we should possess as Christians:

- Put off falsehood and speak the truth
- In your anger, do not sin
- Do not let the sun go down while you are still angry
- Steal no longer
- Do not let unwholesome talk come out of your mouth (it grieves the Holy Spirit)
- Get rid of all bitterness, rage, anger, brawling (a noisy fight, especially in a public place), slander (a false and malicious statement that damages somebody's reputation) and every form of malice (the intention or desire to cause harm or pain to somebody)
- Be kind and compassionate to one another
- Forgive each other
- Live a life of love
- No hint of fornication, impurity or greed

- No obscenity, foolish talk or coarse joking
- Give thanks
- Do not be partners with immoral, impure or greedy persons
- Have nothing to do with fruitless deeds of darkness, but rather reprove (expose) them
- Be very careful how you live, and make the most of every opportunity to live wisely
- Do not be foolish, but understand God's will
- Do not get drunk on wine
- Be filled with the Spirit
- Sing and make music in your heart to the Lord, giving thanks for everything
- Submit to one another out of reverence for Christ
- Wives, submit to husbands as to the Lord
- Husbands, love your wives as Christ loved the church and gave Himself up for her to make her holy, cleansing her by washing with water through the Word
- Wives must respect husbands
- Children obey parents; honor father and mother
- Fathers, do not provoke your children, but bring them up in the training and instruction of the Lord
- Slaves, obey your earthly masters with respect and fear; wholeheartedly as if serving the Lord, not men.
- Masters, treat your slaves in the same way; do not threaten them
- Be strong in the Lord
- Put on the full armor of God

The books of Colossians, Thessalonians, Timothy, Titus, James and Peter also have many instructions and admonitions on developing Godly character.

Please read Handouts # 7 - 8 on Character. Take the self inventory and evaluation test. How did you do?

****

REVIEW

UNDERSTANDING CHRISTIAN STANDARDS AND PRINCIPLES

1. What does it mean to love another person?
   _____
   _____

2. Give an example of how you showed love toward someone who did not love you:
   _____
   _____
   _____

3. Is it necessary for us to forgive in order to be forgiven? Yes ___ No ___. What is the scriptural reference for your answer? _____

4. List ways in which we can show our humility towards others.
   _____
   _____
   _____

5. What does it mean to repent?
   _____
   _____

6. Have you denied yourself something lately for the cause of Christ? If yes, explain:
   _____
   _____

7. Name three characteristics that a Christian should exhibit and why:
   _____
   _____
   _____
   _____

CHAPTER 6

WHAT HAPPENS WHEN I FALL?

Sometimes because of our failings, our minds think we have fallen beyond reach of the Holy Spirit. We somehow think that God is so disappointed with us that we are ashamed to come back before Him. We lose touch with Him because of our guilt and shame. We think that God did not know what we were going to do before we did it. He knew what we were going to do when He called us; and yet He still called us. It is not God who leaves us; we leave the presence of God and become restless wanderers (Genesis 4:12). What happened? We were enticed by Satan, tempted, and fell into sin.

Genesis 4:7 (NIV, emphasis mine) says "If you do what is right, will you not be accepted? But if you do not do what is right, sin is crouching at your door; it desires to have you, **but you must master it.**" That was a complete revelation to me. We must master sin. How can we fight against Satan and master sin? Only by the blood of Jesus and our confession of faith. Revelation 12:11 states, *"And they overcame him by the blood of the Lamb, and by the word of their testimony."*

We must persevere under trial and tribulation. Our faith is tested in trials and these **must** come so that we can become strong and whole, not lacking anything. I believe trials expose our weaknesses (in body and character) so that we know what to pray for and in what to exercise faith. When our faith is exercised, we are made stronger and it is developed. The testing of our faith develops perseverance and perseverance **must** finish its perfect work (James 1:2-4). As we press through trials, we gain experience in how to handle the trial so that it is not so intimidating. We begin to have more faith in God to handle the situation. As our faith grows, we are able to rest in Him. The more we are able to rest in Him through the trial, the more He is able to work on our behalf. He cannot rescue (or save) us when we are too fearful and fitful. Sometimes He has to render us more helpless in order to save us. Rest in God means faith in God.

> When fear has no power over us, faith goes into action. As faith grows, we become mature and complete.

We are able to persevere through trials by having faith that God will see us through; the trial no longer has power to shake us. So when the trial and tests come, learn quickly where weaknesses lie, confess, and pray for change.

Work out imperfections in faith and rest in God until the battle is over. Keep the faith; faith becomes bigger, the trial becomes smaller, the enemy flees, and you are more than a conqueror! Rejoice in the fact that another battle is won!

James 1:13-15 says *"Let no man say when he is tempted, I am tempted of God: for God cannot be tempted with evil, neither tempteth he any man: But every man is tempted, when he is drawn away of his own lust, and enticed. Then when lust hath conceived, it bringeth forth sin: and sin, when it is finished, bringeth forth death."*

I have learned that I cannot be double-minded about God's will and His way. I must accept it as it is or not at all. When I fail at obeying Him implicitly, it is not His fault when I do not receive what I ask for. The fault is mine and mine alone. No matter who participated with me in the deception or the sin. I cannot even blame Satan. Even though Satan tempts us to sin and entices us with desires that battle within us, he does not make us sin. I was tempted when, by my own evil desire, I was dragged away and enticed. After desire was conceived in me, it gave birth to sin. I set my mind on the sinful nature living in me and its desires; I succumbed to my sinful nature and took action based on its desires.

Romans 8:5 says *"For they that are after the flesh do mind the things of the flesh; but they that are after the Spirit the things of the Spirit."* So, I am led by my sinful nature and not by the Spirit of God when I am tempted and fall into sin. The sin causes me to be led away from the presence of the Lord. I then become a restless wanderer who disobeyed God. I may have to suffer the consequences of my own sin, one of which is not being in the presence of the Lord, because His Spirit cannot dwell in darkness. I have to be cleansed and restored for His Spirit to dwell in me. That takes confession, repentance, prayer, and self denial.

> 1 Corinthians 10:13 says *"There hath no temptation taken you but such as is common to man: but God is faithful, who will not suffer you to be tempted above that ye are able; but will with the temptation also make a way to escape, that ye may be able to bear it."* Note: We need to take the way of escape provided for us.

1 John 1:9 says *"If we confess our sins, he is faithful and just to forgive us our sins, and to cleanse us from all unrighteousness."*

The Standards of Christian Conduct

I had a friend say to me once, "When I start to pray, my mind wanders and I can't concentrate on my prayer." That seemed foreign to me until one day I was praying, and my mind began to wander. I wanted so desperately for my prayer to be effectual and fervent, but my conscience was not clear, and I could not pray. I knew that I had a bitter root of resentment, anger, pride, and unmet needs.

As I prayed, my mind would wander to events that took place during the day, what someone said to me or to someone else that may have been offensive. It wandered to what I needed to do that day or what happened last night. Because I wanted to pray better, I would stay on my knees for long periods of time, with a few words here and there in prayer to God and several minutes of thinking of other things, until I finally ended the inadequate prayer with "Lord have mercy on me!" My mind would also wander when I read the Holy Bible. I would read words over and over because I was not paying attention to what I read. I was thinking of other things. I read on a little further and my mind wandered again until I ended the poor excuse for Bible study and went on with my day.

Eventually, I realized that when I prayed, I was not talking with the Lord at all, but trying to recite a rote prayer I had said many times before or heard before. Sometimes we are unable to pray because our minds are not clear. Peter says in 1 Peter 4:7 (NIV), *"The end of all things is near. Therefore be clear minded and self-controlled so that you can pray."* When our minds are not clear and we are not exercising self-control, it is hard for us to pray.

I started to write down things that were on my mind. I wrote everything I could think of that was troubling me, or that I was worrying about, all things about myself that I was in denial of (e.g. pride, selfish ambitions, resentments, and bitterness). I wrote what people had done to me and how I felt about it. When I had taken a look within, I saw what was in me that needed prayer. I cleared my conscience of things that were hidden in me. I stopped reciting and began to talk to the Lord about what was going on in my life (as if He did not know). I confessed sins, my anger and resentments, and prayed that He forgive my wrongs and create in me a clean heart and renew a righteous spirit in me. I prayed that He would forgive me for allowing fear to stifle me and show me how to conquer my fears and live for Him. I confessed that I had been bitter, prideful, and selfish (wanting things my own way and in my own time).

I realized that He always provided for me and, regardless of whether I had what I wanted, He always provided what I needed. I told the Lord that "He completed me" and had a release of tears that had been trapped inside that I was too stubborn to let go. As a child cries himself to sleep, I laid down because I was just exhausted after that cry. It was then that the Lord began to speak to me. He spoke to me through His

Word (which I had stored in my heart) about restoration of the spirit and renewal of the mind as follows (emphases mine):

Romans 12:2 - "*...**be not conformed to this world: but be ye transformed by the renewing of your mind**, that ye may prove what is that good, and acceptable and perfect will of God.*"

Hebrews 12:15 (NIV) - "*See to it that no one falls short of the grace of God and that no **bitter root** grows up to cause trouble and defile many.*"

I had let bitterness, lust, anger, and unforgiveness seep into my soul. These things were warring against my soul, causing separation and wandering from God (1Peter 2:11; Genesis 4:16). I needed to have my soul restored.

> The Holy Spirit connects with and influences our human spirit (in our hearts), the human spirit influences our mind, the mind influences our emotions, our emotions influence our will, and our will influences our body and tells it what to do.

When I feel that my connection with the Holy Spirit has been compromised in any way, I must work to have my mind refreshed and renewed so that I do not fall further into sin and begin to think that the world's ways make sense and are realistic, and God's ways are "idealistic." Nothing can be further from the truth. My spiritual muscle (faith) has become weak. I must exercise my faith to make it strong again. How? By restoring the connection to my source of strength, the Holy Spirit. It can be a short or long process depending on how far away I fell from grace and how long it has been since I was Spiritually connected.

One way to exercise our faith muscle is to pray and read God's Word, and confess with our mouths that Jesus is Lord and can handle any trial we may be going through. This will seem hard and may appear fruitless at first, but <u>do not quit</u>. We cannot quit at the first sign of distraction or trouble; we **must** press our way through pain and confusion (refer to section on Meet the Press in chapter 9). We must continue to pray all during the day, continue to set aside time for Bible study and meditation (early in the mornings, if possible). Unplug the phone to keep distractions down; family and friends can leave a message and you can call them back after devotion time. Continue to learn scripture, especially those relating to your issues. Persevere under pressure and trials, confusion and pain. You **must** press through difficulty.

> As we continue spending quality time with God, reading our Bibles, praying and fasting, we will see a gradual change in our attitude towards our problems, strength in our inner man, and a restoration of our souls. Power comes and we will begin again to trust in God for all our needs.

When there is a setback, say aloud, "Lord I still trust you!" and continue to be obedient every day to the Word you learned. Stay connected to the Holy Spirit at all costs. It is vitally important to set time aside daily to spend quality time with God.

You will find that He will again begin to speak to you (whether in dreams, visions, through other people, or through His Word). Persevere in reading all you can about Jesus Christ and continue to pray and confess His Word constantly. A gradual change will again take place in your spirit as you connect with the Holy Spirit.

Jesus told a parable in Matthew 12:43-45 about when an evil (or unclean) spirit comes out of a man. He said it goes through dry places looking for rest and doesn't find it. It says, "I will return to the house I came out of." When it arrives, it finds the house empty, clean and in order. Then it goes in and it takes with it seven spirits that are more evil than itself, and they all go in and live. The man finds that he is worse than before.

Let us be careful that we do not ignore the leading of the Holy Spirit when He is compelling us to return to Him and to the Lord. We will fall sometimes in our walk with God. If we confess our sins, God cleanses us of all unrighteousness. When He does cleanse us and we are put back in order, let us continue to be filled with the Holy Spirit and continue to exercise our faith by reading and hearing the Word of God for Spiritual growth. Otherwise, we allow Satan to return us to our former sins and our condition will be worse than it was before.

> When we fall, we know what to do...confess, ask for forgiveness, and repent. We need to allow the Lord to pick us up, dust us off and put us back on the right path. We will continue in His Word so we may be free indeed to live and love as the true disciples we are!!

HOW DO I HANDLE FEELINGS OF GUILT AND SHAME?
(Guilt vs. Conviction: the truth, the whole truth, and nothing but the truth)

GUILT:

In order to understand how to handle our feelings of guilt and shame, we first need to understand what guilt is. The devil tries to make us feel guilty and ashamed when we stumble in some way or have bad thoughts. Those bad feelings make us fall further into sin by making us fear, then fall into unbelief. With our faith lessened, we may think things are one way and when they are actually not that way. We may do or say something that we should not do or say. Remember that the feeling of guilt is only that — a feeling. Feelings can change depending on the circumstances. Truth does not change. To convict means to prove or find guilty. So a conviction is a finding of guilt. To be guilty is to be deserving of punishment because of the violation of a law. There are different degrees of guilt depending on a person's knowledge, involvement, and motive. The truth either convicts or sets free.

> In a court of law, a finding of guilt is a conviction; a finding of innocence (free from guilt or "not guilty") sets you free. Just because you are accused of guilt or made to feel guilty, does not mean you are guilty and will be convicted.

Satan is the great accuser and will try to make you feel guilty and commit a sin or further sin based on your feelings. Remember, he is a liar and the father of lies (false witness; perjurer). When you are feeling guilty, those messages that make you feel guilty are from Satan. When you are convicted of guilt, those messages are from the Holy Spirit. The Holy Spirit convicts the world of guilt in regard to sin as explained in John 16:8.

The Holy Spirit does not say "Maybe you are guilty and maybe you are not." Either you are guilty or you are innocent. So when you are feeling guilty about something and you feel bad because maybe you should not have done this or that, and you <u>feel</u> guilty and torn, these messages are from the devil designed to confuse you. You say "I don't know if I should have done that or maybe I should do this, but I'm not sure." You feel torn and you feel bad. Know that it is the work of the devil to make you feel that way. Realize that he is doing his job – accusing you before God day and night (Rev 12:10). He is trying to destroy you or make you destroy yourself. It is not the work of God.

CONVICTION:

The whole truth is needed for a conviction. Usually this conviction will be immediate if you are a mature Christian because the Holy Spirit is at work. You say to yourself, "I <u>know</u> I should not have done that" or "I <u>know</u> I was wrong." This is conviction and is from the Holy Spirit. When you are convicted, the truth convicted you.

If you are unsure of the truth or need more information, go back to the source, the law, or the Holy Bible; or you may consult your representative, advisor, and mediator (Jesus). If, after gathering all the truth, you find you are actually wrong (convicted), do not deny the truth, but confess. Your representatives or mediators (Christ/The Holy Spirit) can appeal to a higher authority (God) to get leniency for you. Your sentencing may be eased by the Judge if you appeal to Him (or make a request for help). Humbling yourself before the Judge helps; appeal in the name of your mediator or representative who has more pull than you with the Judge. In Christ, we have a complete pardon for sins because He paid the price for our sins. Our favor with God is restored because our representative found favor with Him.

> As Christians, we know when we sin or fall short of God's glory because we are familiar with His laws (they are written in our hearts). we are convicted in our spirit because we have grieved the Holy Spirit of God that is in us. Because of our love and respect for God and our understanding of the price His Son paid for us, we are not able to continually sin.

Jesus said, "*If you continue in my word, then are ye my disciples indeed; and ye shall <u>know</u> the truth, and the truth shall make you free*" (John 8:31-32). 1 John 1:9 states, "*If we confess our sins, he is faithful and just to forgive us our sins, and to cleanse us from all unrighteousness.*" The adage, "Confession is good for the soul," rings true here because the soul is restored in truth. And even if we must suffer the consequences of our sin, we know that we are still forgiven by the Lord and we can start afresh in our souls and inner being. We are released from guilt and shame and can go on with our lives in righteousness. We should no longer look to the past (to the days we were in sin), but look to the present that is wiped clean and consider ourselves forgiven from the moment we confessed our sin and repented from the wrong doing of which we were convicted.

Romans 8:1-4 (NIV) states:

> *"Therefore, there is now no condemnation for those who are in Christ Jesus, because through Christ Jesus the law of the Spirit of life set me free from the law of sin and death. For what the law was powerless to do in that it was weakened by the sinful nature, God did by sending his*

own Son in the likeness of sinful man to be a sin offering. And so he condemned sin in sinful man, in order that the righteous requirements of the law might be fully met in us, who do not live according to the sinful nature but according to the Spirit."

Do not continue to remind yourself of the sin or allow others to continue to bring it up in your face. Tell them "Yes, I was convicted of that crime/sin, but that is in my past. I am now set free of any wrong doing and am no longer guilty. I am a new man/woman in the sight of God." Small victories restore confidence; exercise your faith and continue to do what is necessary for your renewal. Continue to study the truth which is your Bible or sword and listen to the counsel of the Holy Spirit.

> If you don't know and understand who you are and what you have, you will not appreciate what you have — you may even abuse it. Go back and remind yourself what the Bible says about you. Receive it, believe it, and move on from your past to a new and exciting future!

Finally, "*draw nigh to God and He will draw nigh to you,*" (James 4:8). "*When you... return to the Lord your God and Father, and obey Him with all your heart and all your soul ...then the Lord your God will restore all your fortunes and have compassion on you ...turn to the Lord your God with all your heart and with all your soul, then the Lord will again make you prosperous,*" (Deut 30:2-10 - NIV).

****

JUSTIFICATION

What does it mean when the Holy Bible refers to *justification* or says that we are justified by faith? That is a good question to ask and a good concept to understand. Easton defines justification as "The judicial act of God, by which he pardons all the sins of those who believe in Christ, and accounts, accepts, and treats them as righteous in the eye of the law."

Romans 5:1-2 states, "*Therefore being justified by faith, we have peace with God through our Lord Jesus Christ: by whom also we have access by faith into this grace wherein we stand, and rejoice in hope of the glory of God.*"

Romans 3:28 states, "*Therefore we conclude that a man is justified by faith without the deeds of the law.*"

Faith in the Lord Jesus Christ reconciles us to God and justifies us before Him. What this means is that though we have sinned, Christ paid the price for our sins so that we would not have to suffer the consequence of sin (wrath of God; eternal punishment). We are justified by faith in Jesus Christ. As long as we keep our faith in Jesus and live for Him, we will continue to be justified before God. The reason is that Christ, through the Holy Spirit, will change our ways and make His ways our ways when we continue in Him.

I have learned that <u>it is vitally important to spend quality time with the Lord (I repeat this often because I cannot stress enough how necessary it is for our growth in the Lord)</u>. As I am praying, reading the Holy Bible, and meditating on God's Word, revelation comes to me through the working of the Holy Spirit and I am led in the way I should go that day, or I am given an answer to a problem I was having. He is gradually changing me into His likeness and I am more at peace here on this earth. I am more centered and I do not let the trials of life get me down as much. I can feel the difference in my attitude and life when I do not spend the time I need with Him. Don't be misled and stray from His presence. Keep priorities straight and be prosperous!

****

MEDIATOR

Mediator, by definition, means a person who is a third party in an agreement, dispute, etc. He works to help each party to resolve an issue or negotiates a settlement. He speaks on behalf of one party or another. He is there for the good of both parties or represents both parties.

1 Timothy 2:5 says, "*For there is one God and one <u>mediator</u> between God and men, the man Christ Jesus,*" (emphasis mine).

Hebrews 9:14-15 says, "*...How much more, then, will the blood of Christ, who through the eternal Spirit offered himself unblemished to God, cleanse our consciences from acts that lead to death, so that we may serve the living God!" For this reason Christ is the <u>mediator</u> of a new covenant, that those who are called may receive the promised eternal inheritance—now that he has died as a ransom to set them free from the sins committed under the first covenant,*" (emphasis mine).

Jesus Christ died so that we may be freed from sin and was raised to life so that we may be justified before God as righteous (Romans 4:25). He did not stop there.

He also became our <u>mediator</u> before God to continue to justify us before God. He also reveals His father to us so that we may experience the love and wisdom of God. What a great sacrifice! What great love He has for us!

Just as Jesus is our mediator, we also can be mediators for others who may need intercession for issues that arise in their lives. An intercessor in the Kingdom prays on someone's behalf for their healing, success, victory, help, etc. If you have ever heard of "intercessory prayer," it is the act of interceding or mediating with the Father on someone else's behalf. We can show our love for someone by praying to the Father for their salvation, growth, victory over sickness, disease, poverty, lack, oppression, or anything else that they need. We are examples of Christ and are like Him when we do as He does on behalf of our fellow man, and especially on behalf of our brothers and sisters in Christ.

****

PERSEVERANCE

"Oh Lord, I just can't take it anymore! This situation is bad and I can't continue to tolerate it! I just can't be around him/her another minute! I can't continue in this ministry, church, job, family, school, mission, marriage, world! This is the last straw! They are on my last nerve! This is too hard for me! I give up — I'll go back to what I know and am used to! I'll go back to that which I am comfortable! This is too much pressure! Where are you, Lord, when I need you?! I can't change myself and you are taking too long to change me! I need you now or I am out!"

Sound familiar? Pressure is not pleasant, worry is woeful, and pain is sometimes too persistent. When we are placed in a position that is not comfortable for us, is hard to do or takes too much effort, we do not <u>feel</u> good about it and we want out of the situation! As stated in the handout "Understanding the Mind," we rebel against what we don't understand and we will eventually reject it. We also rebel against what does not feel good mentally or physically.

I remember feeling uncomfortable in a job situation and I did not feel it was necessary for God to allow me to be in it. I was working for an unsupportive boss and I rebelled against what he said at every turn. I was performing duties that did not make sense to me. Sometimes I did not do what I was told because it was simply, in my opinion, the wrong thing to do. I didn't really care because this was a temporary duty station, and I would be going back to my permanent position soon. I had no help with some of the duties that were assigned to me and other co-workers did not help because they felt I should not be in the position anyway. Some resented my being there. I thought of one assignment given to me as unbearable and overwhelming.

I was responsible for coordinating a campaign for the entire agency and a smaller agency with no experience and very little help. I muddled through the assignment with resentment and indifference.

I did the best I could do with the assignment as far as completing assigned tasks, but I was just not good with coordinating people. This was necessary for the campaign to be a success. I was so afraid that the campaign would fail that I completed the major part of the assignment and then told my manager that I was not the one for this job.

When I returned to my permanent position, I learned a valuable lesson in persevering. God had been with me through the entire project. He would tell me when someone was going to come against me and when something was not going to happen right and that I would have to deal with the situation. It was all too overwhelming for me and I just was not comfortable in that situation, so I quit. I lost out on getting a promotion because I was not ready. I told myself I did not want it anyway, but I would be so much further in my career had I persevered through that trial. That experience, however, made me stronger. I began to deal with situations and people in a more assertive way. He told me how to do it! I was just too afraid to do it. I wanted out!

Since that time, I decided to not quit so easily when things got too hard or when the pressure came. I learned that God was not trying to hurt me, but to grow me. When it is said, "These trials come to make me strong," it is the truth. Sometimes God withholds what we ask for because we are not ready. Sometimes another person involved is not ready. Learn and grow from your trials and trust that God knows what He is doing and is working things out for our good. Now I have learned to say, "Lord I trust you." Even when it does not seem like things are going right or I just received a bad report, I say "Lord I still trust you." I endeavor to do what thus says the Lord and leave the results to Him.

Sometimes we are with someone or in a certain church or ministry and we don't understand everything about them or it. Sometimes they get on our last nerve. Is it time to cut and run? No. It is time to pray and let the Lord bring answers. Maybe the Lord is trying to get us to see our own selfish or unyielding ways. Maybe He just wants us to show mercy or kindness to our brother or sister instead of **us** always wanting kindness and mercy. OK, things are not right in the ministry or relationship or whatever the assignment may be. The person or leaders are making unwise decisions and you can't take it anymore. This is just not what you are used to. Have you ever thought to call and talk to or sit and talk to the person before you cut and run? Maybe things can be resolved if you bring up things that have not been thought of previously. More often than not, God wants us to improve our love walk with others.

Pray to God for clarity and direction first and then, if you are led, have a discussion with the one who vexes you.

> Persevere under relational trials as hard as you would persevere under situational trials.

As stated before, James 1:2 says, *"My brethren, count it all joy when ye fall into divers temptations; knowing this, that the trying of your faith worketh patience. But let patience have her perfect work, that ye may be perfect and entire, wanting nothing."*

What we consider trials, hardship, and pressure is what God uses to grow us up. These trials are just a test of our faith and maturity. God is making sharp and ready instruments out of us so that we may be useful in His Kingdom. Don't run away from a challenge; instead, grow from it and keep pressing! It will get easier not as it changes, but as we change. **See chapter 9 – Pressing Toward the Mark.**

It is stated in 1 Peter 1:3-7 (NIV, emphasis mine), *"Praise be to the God and Father of our Lord Jesus Christ! In His great mercy He has given us new birth into a living hope through the resurrection of Jesus Christ from the dead, and into an inheritance that can never perish, spoil, or fade—kept in heaven for you, who through faith are shielded by God's power until the coming of the salvation that is ready to be revealed in the last time. In this you greatly rejoice, <u>though now for a little while you may have had to suffer grief in all kinds of trials. These have come so that your faith—of greater worth than gold, which perishes even though refined by fire—may be proved genuine and may result in praise, glory and honor when Jesus Christ is revealed."</u>*

Please read over "Affirmations" in handout #9 (Chapter 11) daily.

****

REVIEW

| WHAT HAPPENS WHEN I FALL? |

1. Do you remember a time when you were "feeling" guilty about something and it turned out that you were innocent? Yes ___ No ___. How did you handle your guilty feelings?

_____
_____
_____

2. Explain the importance of telling the truth. Give scriptural references:

_____
_____
_____

3. Explain the difference between feeling guilty and conviction:

_____
_____
_____
_____

4. Explain justification:

_____
_____
_____

5. What are ways that Jesus mediates for us as Christians?

_____
_____
_____

6. Describe a time when you fell and what you did to be restored:

_____
_____
_____

CHAPTER 7

DEALING WITH FELLOW CHRISTIANS/ UNBELIEVERS/ENEMIES

Sometimes it will be difficult to deal with the very persons that we should identify with the most — our fellow believers. All are not the same and all who wear the label are not truly sincere about their calling. Also, we as believers can become numb and religious; doing things mechanically out of duty rather than out of love. It is a trick of the enemy, but we won't fall for the devil's trap! There are times when we just do not agree and we must learn how to handle different situations with our brothers and sisters in Christ.

RESOLVING CONFLICT WITH CHURCH MINISTRIES

I remember going to church one Sunday to work in the Children's Ministry. I was a teacher for the 6th – 8th grade students. I did not want to go because often there were not enough teachers to cover all the classes, there were not enough materials to conduct class properly, no one was there to lead the praise and worship time before classes began, and the kids were sometimes too active and disruptive. I was growing weary in well doing, to say the least. I could tell that other teachers and helpers were feeling the same. No matter how much the leadership team met to discuss problems, it seemed like nothing changed. We began to grumble and complain about the state of the Children's Ministry and some stopped coming. The call to minister to the children was marred by our feelings of resentment and displeasure. We began to speak to each other in a less than loving way and distance ourselves from those who we felt were not pulling their share of the load. Needless to say, we were digressing in our relationship with each other. We were allowing the enemy to come between us. The ministry began to suffer and we lost leaders to other ministries and sometimes to other churches. I was moved to another area of the same ministry. I did not pursue the change myself, but was led, I believe, by God to where He wanted me to be for that season.

What can we do in adverse circumstances? Prayer is the answer. We can either pray alone, or with other ministry members who have the heart and desire to keep the ministry going. We can speak with the elders of the ministry or church individually or as a group. We can <u>decide not to argue, grumble or complain any longer (Philippians 2:14)</u>. We can brainstorm about possible solutions, and if we have no authority to make certain changes, we can change what we can. Be prayerful and resist judging others. We never know what a person may be going through. <u>If we blame others, we must first be without blame; if we rebuke others, we must first be without behavior or action worthy of rebuke</u>. Righteous communication is the key to resolving conflicts. Many times as Christians we are hesitant about talking to leadership or those over which we are leaders for fear of being looked at differently, being judged, or of being moved from our position as leaders. In these situations, if we remember individually to rely on God alone to be our strength, our help, and source, we will be able to get through conflict in the church by resolving it His way, no matter the consequence.

Confess to church leaders any area where you may have fallen short and suggest ways you or the ministry will make improvements. Don't be afraid to address areas of concern. Be self controlled, prayerful and alert when dealing with conflict because we know that our enemy is at work trying to make the ministry of the gospel of no effect.

2 Timothy 2:14-16 (NIV) states, *"Keep reminding God's people of these things. Warn them before God against quarreling about words; it is of no value, and only ruins those who listen. Do your best to present yourself to God as one approved, a worker who does not need to be ashamed and who correctly handles the word of truth. Avoid godless chatter, because those who indulge in it will become more and more ungodly.*

2 Timothy 2:23-26 (NIV, emphasis mine) says, *"Don't have anything to do with foolish and stupid arguments, because you know they produce quarrels. And the Lord's servant must not be quarrelsome but must be kind to everyone, able to teach, not resentful. Opponents must be <u>gently</u> instructed, in the hope that God will grant them repentance leading them to a knowledge of the truth, and that they will come to their senses and escape from the <u>trap of the devil</u>, who has taken them captive to do his will."*

> If all fails, just keep your conscience clear about your role and assignment in the ministry and as a child of God. Do your part and God will do His part. If it is time to move on, He will show you that too. Only leave the choice to Him; don't make the choice because of your own frustrations and carnal thoughts.

The church institution has come a long way from what it was intended to be when first established. It should be a place of refuge and reconciliation. Instead of being God's house, some have become a place of employment for men who administer "church" covenant and teach the traditions of men. How many Christians feel they can take their matters of disagreement to the church and receive good, sound, Biblical decisions? Congregations have become a heavy burden to church pastors and leaders. I believe the return to the righteous place God would have us be starts in the heart of each individual believer. Thank God that He has made a way for each of us to go beyond the curtain into the inner sanctuary to find our High Priest for ourselves. When we have done what we are called to do in ministry, we should turn and help those who may be struggling. We should be such good examples of Christ that our influence will change others.

RESOLVING PERSONAL CONFLICT

On a more personal level, when you are dealing with a Christian friend or relative and there is some tension in the relationship, you must deal with that too. It is not right to just avoid that person without first trying to resolve the conflict or disagreement between you.

> Be careful not to hide unforgiveness or bitterness in your heart. Your walk and your relationship with God and your brother or sister in Christ will be hindered.

Jesus says in Matthew 5:22-24, *"But I say unto you, that whosoever is angry with his brother without a cause shall be in danger of the judgment: and whosoever shall say to his brother, Raca [Aramaic term of contempt], shall be in danger of the council: but whosoever shall say, thou fool, shall be in danger of hell fire. Therefore if thou bring thy gift to the altar, and there rememberest that thy brother hath ought against thee; leave there thy gift before the altar, and go thy way; first be reconciled to thy brother, and then come and offer thy gift."*

So we see that it is important to God that we are reconciled with our brothers and sisters in Christ. The above scriptures tell us what we are to do.

Also, Matthew 18:15-17 says, *"Moreover if thy brother shall trespass against thee, go and tell him his fault between thee and him alone: if he shall hear thee, thou hast gained thy brother. But if he will not hear thee, then take with thee one or two more, that in the mouth of two or three witnesses every word may be established. And if he shall neglect to hear them, tell it unto the church: but if he neglect to hear the church, let him be unto thee as an heathen man and a publican."*

We must understand that we were put here on this earth to relate to and love other people. The people we will have the closest relationships with are our fellow believers; therefore, it is important to know how to develop friendships with them. With some it is very easy because of their kind, loving, open and real spirits; with others it is not so easy.

The Holy Bible says in John 13:34-35 [Jesus speaking], *"A new commandment I give unto you, That ye love one another; as I have loved you, that ye also love one another. By this shall all men know that ye are my disciples, if ye have love one to another."*

1 Peter 1:22 states, *"Seeing ye have purified your souls in obeying the truth through the Spirit unto unfeigned love of the brethren, see that ye love one another with a pure heart fervently."*

1 Peter 3:8 (NIV) says, *"Finally, all of you, live in harmony with one another; be sympathetic, love as brothers, be compassionate and humble."*

1 Peter 4:8-9 states (NIV), *"Above all, love each other deeply, because love covers over a multitude of sins. Offer hospitality to one another without grumbling."*

Notice that Jesus does not request that we love each other as disciples, He **commands** us to love. He says, "As I have loved you, you **must** love one another." Disciples loving one another is serious business; it is the mark of discipleship. Jesus says by this all men will know that you are my disciples, if you love one another. So we may as well accept that we must do it and learn how to do it in a way that is sincere and pure.

So how do you love someone that you can hardly stand, even if he/she is your fellow brother/sister in Christ? One way is to check your own heart first. Are you harboring bitterness, resentments, anger, jealousy, covetousness, fear, or the like in your heart towards this person or what this person represents? You may see in this person some things you dislike in yourself. Many times we hate things about another person that we hate in ourselves and we hold resentments towards that person without even realizing it, or that person may have triggered something in us from our past by a mannerism or word and we resent them because of it. We will then rebel against them or reject them, their teaching, or authority. These things are strongholds within <u>us</u> that need to be dealt with **before** we can deal with anyone else. It is a part of crucifying self or the flesh.

If we see one of our fellow Christians and think something bad about them within ourselves or wish something other than their well being, we are in the flesh and need to check ourselves and get back with the Lord to heal whatever is in us that is not like Him (anger, lusts, bitterness, etc.). The thing that provoked us to anger or resentment has to be healed first. It may seem hard, but it can be done. We must have healed "the thing" in us that is aroused by his or her presence. We do not want the enemy to have a foothold by not dealing with these issues within us that are provoked by someone else. We have to be unmoved by that person or thing.

> 1 Peter 5:8 says, *"Be sober, be vigilant; because your adversary the devil, as a roaring lion, walketh about, seeking whom he may devour: whom resist stedfast in the faith, knowing that the same afflictions are accomplished in your brethren that are in the world."*

It can only be done with the help of the Lord and He will help us in our infirmities and intercede for us with the Father. Secondly, when it is appropriate (after you have judged your own heart, confessed your own sin, prayed for your deliverance, and have resolved within yourself that you will change your bad ways — or repented), do the following:

1. Call your brother or sister in Christ and ask if the two of you (or three, etc.) can talk. Maybe you can meet for lunch, coffee, or maybe the phone call will suffice.

2. Say to your brother or sister, "I know that there is some tension between the two of us and I would like to try resolve whatever it is that is keeping us from being friends or working together."

3. Tell your brother or sister in Christ what was said or done to cause you to feel offended or hurt.
Confess to them your part in the conflict that was not right (something said or done) and ask for forgiveness. If possible, try to rectify the wrong.

4. If your brother or sister in Christ is willing to listen, agrees that this issue should be resolved, and is willing to work with you to resolve it, you have won over your brother or sister.

5. If your brother or sister is unwilling or you are unable to resolve the issue, suggest that you talk to another trusted Christian brother or sister who has no knowledge of the situation for possible resolution.

6. If there is still no resolution, and if your brother or sister has <u>sinned</u> against you and you feel the issue is serious enough for further pursuit, ask if they would not mind going for counseling at your church.

7. If they agree, schedule a counseling session. If not, avoid your brother or sister and pray for them. Let them know you are willing to get counseling if they change their minds.

Per Titus 3:9 (NIV), *"... warn a divisive person once, and then warn him a second time. After that, have nothing to do with him. You may be sure that such a man is warped and sinful; he is self condemned."*

8. Do not repeat the offense to anyone else, but be prayerful and discerning.

Proverbs 17:9 states, *"He that covereth a transgression seeketh love; but he that repeateth a matter separateth friends."*

Proverbs 19:11(NIV) states, *"A person's wisdom yields patience; it is to one's glory to overlook an offense."*

Sometimes, in order to love someone, you must take your eyes off of that person and put them on God. Pray to God concerning the person and your relationship with them. The Lord will show you things about that person (maybe something that happened in their childhood; maybe the abuser was abused himself or herself and knows no other way). Seeing why another person may be behaving in an ungodly manner will help us understand the reason for such behavior and cause us to be a little more merciful towards them. You may be used by the Lord to help break the cycle and restore your brother or sister to love. You never know how or with whom God wants to use you. Unblock the channel by getting rid of self.

Finally, know that you have done your part in resolving the matter. Let God handle the rest. When we are at the point where the thing or person does not affect us in a negative way anymore, we are healed, and are able to face them without fear, resentments or anger. We have grown spiritually and are able to address them with love.

Read over Colossians chapter 3:1 – 4:6 for instructions on dying to self and loving others.

****

WHO IS MY NEIGHBOR? DO I TREAT EVERYONE THE SAME?

The Holy Bible tells us how we should treat our neighbor, our enemy, and our brothers and sisters in Christ. It gives specific instructions on how to treat each. Do we treat our neighbor the same as we treat our enemy? Or, do we treat our brother the same as we treat our neighbor? Do we love each other the same?

Let's explore further —

Neighbor

1. When asked by an expert in the law "And who is my neighbor?", Jesus replied by telling a parable about a man who fell into the hands of robbers and three who encountered him in Luke 10:29-35. The neighbor was determined to be the one <u>who had mercy</u> on the robbery victim. The expert in the law was told to "Go and do likewise."

2. My neighbor therefore, is the one who has mercy on me, and I am a neighbor to the one on whom I have mercy.

Enemy

1. In Matthew 5:43-49 (NIV), Jesus explains that we should love our enemies instead of hating them, as was once thought. He further explains that we should do this so that <u>we</u> may be sons of our Father in heaven. He states that "if you love those who love you, what reward will you get; and if you greet only your brothers, what are you doing more than others?" He says "be perfect, therefore, as your heavenly Father is perfect."

2. My enemy does not wish me well. He may hate me and seek to harm me, but the Lord says to love my enemies. According to Micah 7:6 – A man's enemies are, at times, members of his "own house."

Brother (Sister) in Christ

1. In Mark 3:32-35, Jesus was told that His mother and brothers were outside looking for Him. At this He asked, *"Who are my mother or my brethren?"* He then stated, *"Whosoever shall do the will of God, the same is my brother, and my sister, and mother."*

2. Jesus makes it plain that not everyone is His brother, sister, or mother. He says my *"My mother and my brethren are these which hear the word of God, and do it."* (Luke 8:21)

3. He referred to the disciples as his brothers and mother (Matt 12:49).

4. Brothers and sisters in Christ are the ones who do the Father's will. They hear the word of God **and** put it into practice.

5. This relationship is the greatest among the three and deserves special attention as shown below. Jesus had a special relationship with His "brothers."

    - 1 John 2:10-11 – *"He that loveth his brother abideth in the light, and there is none occasion of stumbling in him. But he that hateth his brother is in darkness, and walketh in darkness, and knoweth not whither he goeth, because that darkness hath blinded his eyes."*

    - 1 John 4:20-21 – *"If a man say, I love God, and hateth his brother, he is a liar: for he that loveth not his brother whom he hath seen, how can he love God whom he hath not seen? And this commandment have we from him, That he who loveth God love his brother also."*

    - Matthew 25:40 – *"And the King shall answer and say unto them, Verily I say unto you, Inasmuch as ye have done it unto one of the least of these my brethren, ye have done it unto me."*

Do we love our neighbor and our enemy the same way? Yes, but our enemy is not going to love us or treat us the same.

Do we love our neighbor the same as we love our brothers (sisters) in Christ? We do good to all people, but **especially** to those who belong to the family of believers (Galatians 6:10).

In conclusion, we should love our neighbor as ourselves; we have mercy on our neighbors. We love our enemy, do good to him, and do not resist him. We depend on God to rescue us from our enemies. We love our brothers (and sisters) "deeply, from the heart," (1 Peter 1:22-NIV).

Complete handout # 10 – Self Evaluation of Mercy and Humility (Chapter 11)

****

SOME OF THE WORST SINNERS ARE SO-CALLED CHRISTIANS

While it is our duty as Christians to love everyone, **especially** the family of believers, we are to also have a discerning spirit about those who say they know Christ and yet continually sin. It is understable for a person who is a new believer to stumble many times before they grow in the Spirit and are changed by perseverance in the Word into mature saints of God. Sometimes, however, people who have been Christians for a long period of time have not matured in the Spirit as they should.

Paul speaks about such persons in 1 Corinthians 3:1-3 (NIV, emphasis mine) in his writings to the church at Corinth. He says, *"Brothers and sisters, I could not address you as people who live by the Spirit but as people who are <u>still worldly— mere infants in Christ</u>. I gave you milk, not solid food, for you were not yet ready for it. Indeed, you are still not ready. You are still worldly. For since there is jealousy and quarreling among you, are you not worldly? Are you not <u>acting like mere humans</u>?"*

If a Christian does not continue in the Word of God, pray, and use discipline in seeking God <u>diligently</u>, they do not mature and very little change is manifested in their lives. They will find that it is hard to come out of the world and may still be caught up in its snare. Christ is not able to work in their lives because they do not allow Him to change them.

Hebrews 5:11-14 (NIV) states, *"We have much to say about this, but it is hard to make it clear to you because you no longer try to understand. In fact, though by this time you ought to be teachers, you need someone to teach you the elementary truths of God's word all over again. You need milk, not solid food!"*

> *"Anyone who lives on milk, being still an infant, is not acquainted with the teaching about righteousness. But solid food is for the mature, who by constant use have trained themselves to distinguish good from evil."*

If we truly believed in God's Son, we would put our life in His hands and be willing to obey God. We would not deliberately continue to sin because Christ lives in us. 1 John 3:6-10 (NIV, emphasis mine) states, *"No one who lives in Him keeps on sinning. No one who continues to sin has either seen Him or known Him. Dear children, do not let anyone lead you astray... <u>No one who is born of God will continue to sin</u>, because God's seed remains in him; <u>he cannot go on sinning</u>, because he has been born of God. <u>This is how we know who the children of God are and who the children of the devil are: Anyone who does not do what is right is not a child of God; nor is anyone who does not love his brother</u>".*

Jesus said himself, when speaking to the Jews in John 8:42-47 (emphasis mine), *"If God were your Father, ye would love me: for I proceeded forth and came from God; neither came I of myself, but he sent me. Why do ye not understand my speech? even because ye cannot hear my word. <u>Ye are of your father the devil, and the lusts of your father ye will do</u>. He was a murderer from the beginning, and abode not in the truth, because there is no truth in him. When he speaketh a lie, he speaketh of his own: for he is a liar, and the father of it. And because I tell you the truth, ye believe me not. Which of you convinceth me of sin? And if I say the truth, why do ye not believe me? <u>He that is of God heareth God's words: ye therefore hear them not, because ye are not of God</u>."*

Jesus also says in Matthew 7:21-23, *"Not everyone that saith unto me, Lord, Lord, shall enter into the kingdom of heaven; but he that doeth the will of my Father which is in heaven. Many will say to me in that day, Lord, Lord, have we not prophesied in thy name? and in thy name have cast out devils? and in thy name done many wonderful works? And then will I profess unto them, I never knew you: depart from me, ye that work iniquity."*

So we see that not everyone who appears to be a believing Christian is actually a true Believer, even some who are able to perform miraculous signs in the name of Jesus. Not every man or woman who enters a pulpit to preach is a true Believer. 1 John 4:1 states, *"Beloved, believe not every spirit, but try the spirits whether they are of God: because many false prophets are gone out into the world."*

Matthew 7:15, 16, 19-20 says, *"Beware of false prophets, which come to you in sheep's clothing, but inwardly they are ravening wolves. Ye shall know them by their fruits... Every tree that bringeth not forth good fruit is hewn down, and cast into the fire. Wherefore by their fruits ye shall know them."*

The fruit of the Spirit, according to Galatians 5:22, is *"love, joy, peace, longsuffering, gentleness, goodness, faith, meekness, temperance."* These characteristics should be exhibited in everyone who calls himself a Christian. If Christ lives in us, we may not be perfected yet, but we will not continuously sin.

If we run across someone who says he/she is a Christian, but deliberately continues to sin, we should be very cautious around this person. We cannot judge the person because we never know how God will work in their lives. They may eventually confess and repent of their ways. We should, however, make a <u>right judgment</u> as to whether we will continue to be in close relationship with them if they continue to sin and not listen to reason. We should pray for them according to 1 John 5:16.

James 5:19-20 states, *"Brethren, if any of you do err from the truth, and one convert him; Let him know, that he which converteth the sinner from the error of his way shall save a soul from death, and shall hide a multitude of sins."*

We must be cautious when trying to restore our brother or sister so that we are not tempted to fall too, as per Galatians 6:1. We may not always immediately discern who is a true Christian because they may exhibit some Christian characteristics, but we should look always for the Spiritual fruit as stated above, pray, and use Spiritual wisdom in our dealings with everyone.

Jesus wants us to not only hear His words, but practice them as explained in Matthew 7:24-27. If we do not persevere in the Word, we will not produce the fruit we need and mature in the Spirit.

****

HOW TO RECOGNIZE AND AVOID THE PHARISEE MENTALITY

The Holy Bible records in Luke 18:9-14 a parable of Jesus about people who are self righteous (righteous in their own eyes), and that judge other people. They think they are better than others, especially those who they consider sinners or beneath them. Jesus warns us not to be prideful and judgmental. The parable reads as follows:

"And he spake this parable unto certain which trusted in themselves that they were righteous, and despised others: Two men went up into the temple to pray; the one a Pharisee, and the other a publican. The Pharisee stood and prayed thus with himself, God, I thank thee, that I am not as other men are, extortioners, unjust, adulterers, or even as this publican. I fast twice in the week, I give tithes of all that I possess.

And the publican, standing afar off, would not lift up so much as his eyes unto heaven, but smote upon his breast, saying, God be merciful to me a sinner."

"I tell you, this man went down to his house justified rather than the other: for every one that exalteth himself shall be abased; and he that humbleth himself shall be exalted."

The Pharisee in this parable was a man who was well versed in the law and administered laws to the people. He had an air of superiority about him and knew he was better than the common publican (tax collector). Pharisees would separate themselves from, and not associate with, common sinners. Tax collectors in those days were, for the most part, receiving too many taxes from the people for their own dishonest gain. They were considered "sinners" (see Luke 19:1-9).

A LOOK AT THE PHARISEE MENTALITY:

- In this case, the Pharisee considered himself better than the "sinner." He was righteous in his own eyes and he thought he pleased God by his religious rituals and by not associating himself with sinners.

  But we see by Jesus' parable that God is not pleased with those who are prideful and not humble. The tax collector confessed that he was a sinner and asked for mercy. He beat his breast and was sorrowful. God honors and exalts the humble rather than the one who exalts himself. The Pharisee mentality is a way of thinking that one is better than others.

- They brag on themselves and are prideful. They are confident in "themselves" or "self" and give credit to themselves for what they have obtained or accomplished.

- They think that God is pleased with them because of their seemingly good works (e.g. paying tithes, feeding the hungry, going to church; they don't smoke or drink, or steal, or kill), and they look down on others who are not like them.

- They are hypocritical (Luke 12:1: Matthew 16:5-12).

Although God is pleased with good works (paying tithes, feeding the hungry, assembling together as saints, etc.) He is not pleased with people who exalt themselves while doing it and look down on other people.

This mentality and attitude is fleshly, carnal, sinful, and should be avoided.

TO AVOID THE PHARISEE MENTALITY REMEMBER:

- <u>As Christians, we put no confidence in the flesh</u>. Paul says in Philippians 3:3-9 (emphasis mine):

"For we are the circumcision, which worship God in the spirit, and rejoice in Christ Jesus, and have <u>no confidence in the flesh</u>. Though I might also have confidence in the flesh. If any other man thinketh that he hath whereof he might trust in the flesh, I more: circumcised the eighth day, of the stock of Israel, of the tribe of Benjamin, an Hebrew of the Hebrews; as touching the law, a Pharisee; concerning zeal, persecuting the church; touching the righteousness which is in the law, blameless.

<u>*But what things were gain to me, those I counted loss for Christ*</u>. *Yea doubtless, and I count all things but loss for the excellency of the knowledge of Christ Jesus my Lord: for whom I have suffered the loss of all things, and do count them but dung, that I may win Christ, And be found in him<u>, not having mine own righteousness, which is of the law, but that which is through the faith of Christ, the righteousness which is of God by faith</u>."*

It is easy, once a person has accepted the Lord as his Savior and begun to live a new life in Christ, to become overly confident in himself and think that because he is a part of the kingdom of God, that he (or she) is better than the "sinner" who has not accepted Christ. For this reason, some have gone on to preach a fire and damnation sermon to unbelievers. And while it is imperative that sinners repent and come into the knowledge of Christ and accept Him as Lord and Savior, and while the time is short, we must not begin to exalt ourselves and become self righteous and act as if our righteousness was of our own doing.

- <u>It is the Lord that makes us righteous</u>; we only accepted the free gift that was offered us. We are being made perfect by the Spirit of God and it is not of our own doing. We have to remember that we were once sinners and are saved by the grace of God. But for the grace of God, we would be lost. We must remain humble before God and have mercy on unbelievers because we know that God does not want anyone to be lost. When we go out into the world and begin to witness to people, we go with the knowledge that God is exalted, and we discipline ourselves under His mighty hand and we do not boast about what we do.

Paul also says in 1 Corinthians 9:25-27 (emphasis mine):

"Every man that striveth for the mastery is temperate in all things. Now they do it to obtain a corruptible crown; but we an incorruptible. I therefore so run, not as uncertainly; so fight I, not as one that beateth the air: But <u>I keep under my body, and bring it into subjection</u>: lest that by any means, when I have preached to others, I myself should be a castaway."

- <u>Do not esteem ourselves, but esteem others</u>. Philippians 2:3-11 states (emphasis mine):

"Let nothing be done through strife or vainglory; but in lowliness of mind <u>let each esteem other better than themselves</u>. Look not every man on his own things, but every man also on the things of others.

<u>Let this mind be in you, which was also in Christ Jesus</u>: Who, being in the form of God, thought it not robbery to be equal with God: But made himself of no reputation, and took upon him the form of a servant, and was made in the likeness of men: And being found in fashion as a man, <u>he humbled himself, and became obedient</u> unto death, even the death of the cross.

<u>Wherefore God also hath highly exalted him</u>, and given him a name which is above every name: That at the name of Jesus every knee should bow, of things in heaven, and things in earth, and things under the earth; And that every tongue should confess that Jesus Christ is Lord, to the glory of God the Father."

DEALING WITH UNBELIEVERS – CAN I BE A WITNESS?

The best way to deal with unbelievers is with love and compassion. Love, because that is what we do. Compassion, because we have all sinned and fallen short of the glory of God. If we remember how we once behaved when we were in darkness, we can understand the ways of an unbeliever.

If you have been a Christian for some time, think back to when you were in the world and not a Christian. How did you feel when a Christian or a so called Christian approached you with church stuff, or mentioned Jesus Christ to you, or invited you to church? If you were like me, you wished that they would just go away. You didn't want to hear all that stuff and you were sick of going to church when your mother made you go back in the day.

Not many in the world want to hear about Jesus; not in the schools, not in the workplace, not in the government, not in the streets, and not in the home. Some think they are doing pretty well without Him, so why should they listen to what they consider your "babble" about Jesus? A person does not care about how much you know about a subject (including the Bible and Christ) until they first see and know how much you care about them.

Again, it is stated in 1 Corinthians 13:1-3 – *"Though I speak with the tongues of men and of angels, and have not charity, I am become as sounding brass, or a tinkling cymbal. And though I have the gift of prophecy, and understand all mysteries, and all knowledge; and though I have all faith, so that I could remove mountains, and have not charity, I am nothing. And though I bestow all my goods to feed the poor, and though I give my body to be burned, and have not charity, it profiteth me nothing."*

You have heard the expression, "meet the people where they are." That is to say, if you are among less fortunate people, or say homeless people, know how to approach them. Do not go around them all dressed up and proper … or do you go around them at all? Are they too far gone to reach? "You know if you give them money they will just go out and buy drugs or booze!" If you have this attitude, just avoid communication with them. You are not ready to witness to them because you have not yet been delivered from the prideful "self" in you. God may even use a person who is homeless to minister to you.

> When we meet people where they are, we allow ourselves to walk in their shoes for a moment. Before you try to present Jesus Christ to the unbeliever, try to see things from their point of view. Talk with them to understand their life and why they believe the way they do.

When we are around unbelievers, we should continue to hold up the standard of God in their presence, and we should not be afraid to be in their presence. We should insulate ourselves against the world, not isolate ourselves from the world.

If we have Christ in us and are clothed in righteousness, it will be apparent to the unbeliever. They will detect a peace about us and will, therefore, feel comfortable around us. If we are too prideful or afraid, then we are not guided by the Spirit of God, because God did not give us the spirit of fear, but of love and of power, and of a sound mind according to 2 Timothy 1:7. You may feel a little nervous or uncomfortable at first, but do not let fear possess you. You may have to return to devotion, consecration, prayer, and fasting before you go to talk to certain unbelievers about Christ. If an unbeliever detects too much fear or pride in us, they will not feel comfortable around us and resist or reject what we are saying to them.

When, however, you feel comfortable that this is who God has sent you to speak to, and you are confident in what to say to the unbeliever, do not be afraid to speak to them. This may be the one soul that God is seeking to come into the fold and do great things in His kingdom.

In John chapter 17, Jesus prays for his disciples; He then prays for those who will believe in Him through their message. So we see that there are people who will become believers through our message. That message must be given to unbelievers so that they may have the opportunity to be one with us.

There are unbelievers, however, who have no interest in Christ or becoming like Him. Their only interest is in self and continuing wicked ways. We are not to try to share Christ with them yet because we would be throwing our "pearls to pigs" so to speak as stated in Matthew 7:6 *"Do not give dogs what is sacred; do not throw your pearls to pigs. If you do, they may trample them under their feet, and turn and tear you to pieces."*

The best thing to do is to turn and go your own way according to Proverbs 4:14-16, *"Do not set foot on the path of the wicked or walk in the way of evildoers. Avoid it, do not travel on it; turn from it and go on your way. For they cannot rest until they do evil; they are robbed of sleep till they make someone stumble."*

<u>Who are the Antichrists?</u>

2 John 1:7 states, *"For many deceivers are entered into the world, who confess not that Jesus Christ is come in the flesh. This is a deceiver and an antichrist."*

He tells us further that if anyone comes to us and does not bring the teaching of Christ, do not take him into your house or welcome him. Anyone who welcomes him shares in his evil work (verses 10-11).

As stated in 1 John 4:2-3 (emphasis mine), *"Hereby know ye the Spirit of God: Every spirit that confesseth that Jesus Christ is come in the flesh is of God: And every spirit that confesseth not that Jesus Christ is come in the flesh is not of God: and this is that spirit of <u>antichrist</u>, whereof ye have heard that it should come; <u>and even now already is it in the world</u>."*

By this we are always able to recognize if we are dealing with someone who is antichrist. (**Note**: antichrist is also spoken of in eschatology as "the man of sin" or "beast" who is to come in end times).

There may come a time when the unbeliever is ready to hear the Word, but until that time, avoid his path. The Lord will guide you to whomever He wants you to minister. We only need to have a discerning spirit to know when to approach and when to retreat. Christ does not force Himself on anyone, but stands at the door and knocks; He waits for us to let Him in.

LOVING MY ENEMIES — SAY WHAT?!!!

As stated above, Jesus says love your enemies and pray for those that persecute you. He says that the reason to do this is so that you may be sons of your Father in heaven. He causes His sun to rise on the evil and the good, and sends rain on the righteous and the unrighteous. Therefore, if we really want to be sons (and daughters) of God, we need to learn to love everyone, even our enemies.

But how do you love someone who has hurt you, stolen from you, disregarded your feelings, attacked your character, disowned you, deceived you, hurt or killed your family, attacked you physically and emotionally, wished the worst on you and spoken all kinds of evil against you? Why would you take care of someone who hates you or has hurt you; someone who has tried to kill, steal from, and destroy you?

Because you are God's; and God is greater than evil, therefore, you are greater than evil. You will have no part in its devices. You will not touch with your hand, mind, or heart what is evil. Let the evil person continue to do what he does, but as for you, you will have no part of it.

> The Holy Bible says in Matthew 6:19-21, *"Lay not up for yourselves treasures upon earth, where moth and rust doth corrupt, and where thieves break through and steal: But lay up for yourselves treasures in heaven, where neither moth nor rust doth corrupt, and where thieves do not break through nor steal: For where your treasure is, there will your heart be also."*

What are heavenly treasures and how do you store them up? I believe heavenly treasures are the rewards we receive because of the good deeds done here on earth; by doing what is good in God's eyes, and treasuring His Word and Way, we are storing good things up for ourselves.

The Holy Bible also says in 1 Peter 3:9, *"Not rendering evil for evil, or railing for railing: but contrariwise blessing; knowing that ye are thereunto called, that ye should inherit a blessing."* (Read the rest of 1 Peter 3:10 - 22).

Romans 12:17-21 says (emphasis mine), *"Recompense [repay] to no man evil for evil. Provide things honest in the sight of all men. If it be possible, as much as lieth in you, live peaceably with all men. Dearly beloved, avenge not yourselves, but rather give place unto wrath: for it is written, Vengeance is mine; I will repay, saith the Lord.* **Therefore if thine enemy hunger, feed him; if he thirst, give him drink: for in so doing thou shalt heap coals of fire on his head.** *Be not overcome of evil, but overcome evil with good."*

Good triumphs over evil! God is good and He conquers evil. So if your enemy is getting the best of you, take it to the Lord. Let Him know what is happening in your heart and what the enemy has done. He will repay him for hurting you; just don't take matters into your own hands or you will be like him yourself. I believe that loving your enemy, and not wishing evil on him, is one way to store up heavenly treasures. This is a good reason to do all we can to love our enemies.

Another reason to love your enemies is that you never know who the Lord is after to turn their hearts towards Him and use them in a mighty way. Take Paul as an example. Before his name was changed to Paul, he was called Saul.

He was a persecutor of the church. He asked for letters from the high priest to the synagogues so that if he found any who belonged to the "Way," he could imprison them. He approved of the stoning of Stephen, one of Jesus' disciples. One day as he was on his way to imprison people, he had an experience with Christ and — in the process — lost his sight. A man named Ananias was told to go lay hands on Saul for him to receive his sight. Ananias didn't want to do it because he knew that Saul was an enemy of all who belonged to Christ. As a matter of fact, Ananias reminded the Lord of that. To this the Lord said in Acts 9:15-16 *"Go thy way: for he is a chosen vessel unto me, to bear my name before the Gentiles, and kings, and the children of Israel: For I will shew him how great things he must suffer for my name's sake."*

What if Ananias decided not to obey the Lord and go to Saul because Saul was an enemy of Christ and he knew that Saul persecuted people like him? It would not have been a good thing. Saul was converted to the "Way" as it was called at that time, his name was changed to Paul, and he became a powerful force for the cause of Christ, establishing many churches and writing about 2/3 of the New Testament.

From this we learn a lesson…Only God can judge a man's (or woman's) heart. He calls those who do not seem to be likely candidates. That is because He knows all and can change hearts. Paul was receptive to his call and went on to do great things in the Kingdom of God. Never resist the Lord's leading to help a person you consider an enemy. God may have great things in store for that person and you will be credited for bringing a sinner to Christ (treasure stored in heaven)!

God Is Not Pleased When We think He Allows Evil People to Prosper

In Malachi chapter 3, the Lord was grieved with the people because of their way of thinking and the harsh things they said against Him. Things like what is stated in verses 14-15, *"Ye have said, 'It is vain to serve God: and what profit is it that we have kept his ordinance, and that we have walked mournfully before the LORD of hosts? And now we call the proud happy; yea, they that work wickedness are set up; yea, they that tempt God are even delivered.'"*

The people had given up on God. Don't be like them, but be like those who feared God; the Lord listened to them. *"A scroll of remembrance was written in His presence concerning those who feared the Lord and honored His name"* (treasures in heaven) according to Malachi 3:16 (NIV). Verses 16 - 18 explain that those who fear the Lord are considered His, and He will spare them. He says, *"You will again see the distinction between the righteous and the wicked, between those who serve God and those who do not."* Chapter 4 explains that *"all arrogant and evildoers will be stubble."* The righteous will trample down the wicked.

We as Christians do not want to be counted among the wicked. Those that take revenge on their enemies are as bad as their enemies using evil tactics to hurt them. That is not the way! Take your hurts and pains to God and let Him handle it. It may not be today, it may not be tomorrow, but rest assured that the Lord will handle all of our enemies. You are doing this for you, not your enemy. You have a place in heaven; your enemy, if he does not change, has a place in the fiery furnace. Settle in your mind that you will not envy the wicked and remember the following verses of scripture:

Proverbs 24:1-2 - *"Be not thou envious against evil men, neither desire to be with them. For their heart studieth destruction, and their lips talk of mischief."*

Proverbs 24:19-20 - *"Fret not thyself because of evil men, neither be thou envious at the wicked; for there shall be no reward to the evil man; the candle of the wicked shall be put out."*

Proverbs 24:17-18 - *"Rejoice not when thine enemy falleth, and let not thine heart be glad when he stumbleth: lest the LORD see it, and it displease him, and he turn away his wrath from him."*

The bottom line is, let the Lord handle the wicked and your enemies. He knows better than us how to get revenge and serve justice on them. We as Christians will continue to allow God to purge the bad from our hearts, so we will not be counted among the wicked.

****

JUDGING vs. RIGHT JUDGMENTS

<u>Judging:</u>

To *judge* means to discern, evaluate and make a decision, criticize or condemn. Jesus states in Matthew 7:1-5, *"Judge not, that ye be not judged. For with what judgment ye judge, ye shall be judged: and with what measure ye mete, it shall be measured to you again. And why beholdest thou the mote that is in thy brother's eye, but considerest not the beam that is in thine own eye? Or how wilt thou say to thy brother, Let me pull out the mote out of thine eye; and, behold, a beam is in thine own eye? Thou hypocrite, first cast out the beam out of thine own eye; and then shalt thou see clearly to cast out the mote out of thy brother's eye."*

In saying this, I believe Jesus is admonishing us to first get our lives right **before** we try to criticize someone else for their wrongdoing, or try to tell someone about their mess. We usually are not qualified to judge another person, because we who judge sin also. It would be to our benefit to continue to allow the Lord to move the sin out of our lives and not judge another person as a sinner, a liar, a thief, a murderer, an adulterer, a homosexual, a whoremonger, or any other label we think to give another person. We are being hypocritical when we do this because, usually, we have sin that is not dealt with in our own lives.

> Romans 2:1 states, *"Therefore thou art inexcusable, O man, whosoever thou art that judgest: for wherein thou judgest another, thou condemnest thyself; for thou that judgest doest the same things."*

James 4:11-12 states, *"Speak not evil one of another, brethren. He that speaketh evil of his brother, and judgeth his brother, speaketh evil of the law, and judgeth the law: but if thou judge the law, thou art not a doer of the law, but a judge. There is one lawgiver, who is able to save and to destroy: who art thou that judgest another?"*

If we do not want to be judged for our sin, we should not judge others. We all have the same Judge who is well able to handle all our sinfulness…and **we are not that Judge**. Also, a lot of times when we judge someone, we are condemning them for what they have done or are doing. Sometimes we have a condescending attitude or tone toward the person like we are better than they (the Pharisee mentality). We should be careful in our attitudes and judgments because we never know when we or someone we love may be in the same situation. If that is the case, we would not want anyone to be condescending or judgmental towards us. Instead, we would want them to speak the truth "in love" to us as written in Ephesians 4:15. We can reprove them privately without judging them and reserve judgment for our Father in heaven. We can condemn the sin and not the sinner (an example of this is in John 8:3-11; Jesus did not condemn the woman caught in adultery, but said to go sin no more).

When we sit in judgment of another, we act as if we have it all together and that one sin (theirs) is worse than another sin (ours). On the contrary, all sin is the same in God's eyes. Per James 2:10-11, *"For whosoever shall keep the whole law, and yet offend in one point, he is guilty of all. For he that said, do not commit adultery, said also, do not kill. Now if thou commit no adultery, yet if thou kill, thou art become a transgressor of the law."* In most cases, we are no better than the one we are judging.

2 Corinthians 5:10 says, *"For we must all appear before the judgment seat of Christ; that every one may receive the things done in his body, according to that he hath done, whether it be good or bad."*

<u>Right Judgments:</u>

Now just because we are not to judge other people, does not mean that we are not to make judgments about a situation or circumstance. Remember to judge also means to *discern*. When we use discernment in making judgments, we are doing a good thing. For example, in Acts 4:5-19, when the rulers, elders, and teachers of the law commanded Peter and John not to speak or teach at all in the name of Jesus, they replied, *"Whether it be right in the sight of God to hearken unto you more than unto God, judge ye. For we cannot but speak the things which we have seen and heard."* In this case, Peter and John had to make a <u>judgment call</u> about whether they would obey God or the elders and teachers of the law. They discerned that it would be wiser to listen to God rather than man. They made a <u>right judgment</u>.

In Luke 7:41-43, Jesus told a parable to Simon. He said, *"There was a certain creditor which had two debtors: the one owed five hundred pence, and the other fifty. And when they had nothing to pay, he frankly forgave them both. Tell me therefore, which of them will love him most? Simon answered and said, I suppose that he, to whom he forgave most. And he said unto him, Thou hast rightly judged."* In this case, Simon had to make a decision about who loved more. He discerned that if a person was forgiven more, he would love more. Jesus told him that he judged correctly or made a <u>right judgment</u>. A judgment is a decision about a circumstance or situation based on your discernment of what is right or wrong. Sometimes a person can make a right judgment or sometimes we judge incorrectly. Whatever the judgment call, we must live with the result.

An example of when a right judgment should be used today is when we are faced with a decision of whether or not to gossip about another person for something they have said or done. We should first investigate to see what it means and seek out the Word of God to see how to handle it. Gossip, according to the Encarta Dictionary, is a conversation about the personal details of other people's lives, <u>whether rumor or fact</u>. The Holy Bible says the following about gossip:

- Proverbs 11:13 – *"A talebearer [gossip] revealeth secrets: but he that is of a faithful spirit concealeth the matter."*
- Proverbs 20:19 – *"He that goeth about as a talebearer [gossip] revealeth secrets: therefore meddle not with him that flattereth with his lips."*
- Proverbs 26:20 – *"Where no wood is, there the fire goeth out: so where there is no talebearer [gossip], the strife ceaseth."*

In deciding not to gossip about a person, we have made a <u>right judgment.</u>

Recently, there have been several situations in which a person in religious leadership has fallen away from grace. Do we condemn that person for what they have done or gossip about the situation? Let's judge the question based on scripture:

First, as we have just pointed out, Matthew 7:1 says that we should not judge others. So we should not make a decision about that person and judge them as a whoremonger, child molester, thief, etc. The Bible says do not do that.

How do we handle questions about the person when someone asks us our opinion? We should just say something like, "This person will have to one day stand before the same judge we all will have to stand before. He/she has a judge, and I am not that judge. Therefore, <u>I</u> do not judge him/her."

Next, we will have to make a <u>judgment call</u> about what we will do as a result of our brother's or sister's sin. This takes prayer and a review of scripture to understand what to do, especially if the person is close to us. As stated previously, the Bible states in Matthew 7:5, *"first cast out the beam out of thine own eye; and then shalt thou see clearly to cast out the mote out of thy brother's eye."* Therefore, if you have sin in your own life, deal with that before you try to tell someone else about their sin.

The Bible also says in James 5:16, *"Confess your faults one to another, and pray one for another, that ye may be healed. The effectual fervent prayer of a righteous man availeth much."*

If you have unconfessed sin in your life, seek out a brother or sister in Christ to ask for prayer. You may wish, depending on the situation and with permission of the Holy Spirit, to talk to the one who has sinned in order to pray for him/her and have that person pray for you. If you are not led to talk to them, do not do it; only continue to pray for them and yourself concerning the sin in both your lives.

Do not call a brother or sister in Christ to pray for someone else's sin saying, "We need to pray for sister or brother so and so." This is unbiblical and leads to gossip. Again, the Bible says in Matthew 18:15 (emphasis mine), *"Moreover if thy brother shall trespass [sin] against thee, go and tell him his fault between <u>thee and him alone</u>,"* not between you and someone else. It says also in Luke 17:3 (emphasis mine), *"Take heed to yourselves: If thy brother trespass <u>against thee</u>, rebuke him; and if he repent, forgive him."* This is a private conversation between you and the one who sins (unless they do not listen to you, then you are to take someone else along with you or take it to the church if they still do not listen, according to Matthew 18:16-17).

> Please note that the person who sinned is always in the conversation. It should not be discussed among other people, for this starts gossip.

So we see that gossiping in not a good thing to do, even if it is done with "good intentions". We should cover each other and not be out to expose each other. We should try to turn the sinner from his/her ways once we have dealt with our own sin. James 5:20 states (emphasis mine), *"Let him know, that he which converteth the sinner from the error of his way shall save a soul from death, and shall <u>hide a multitude of sins</u>"*. 1 Peter 4:8 states, *"And above all things have fervent charity [love] among yourselves: for charity shall <u>cover the multitude of sins</u>,"* (emphasis mine).

In some cases, however, when our brother or sister does not listen to us or the church, we have to make a <u>judgment call</u> about whether we should continue to be around them. Sometimes we must separate from them and go our own way if they persist in sin, do not repent, and continue to be divisive. Matthew 18:17 states, *"And if he shall neglect to hear them, tell it unto the church: but if he neglect to hear the church, let him be unto thee as an heathen man and a publican."*

Titus 3:10 (NIV) states, *"Warn a divisive person once, and then warn them a second time. After that, have nothing to do with them. You may be sure that such people are warped and sinful; they are self-condemned."*

Finally, James 2:12 states, *"Speak and act as those who are going to be judged by the law that gives freedom, because judgment without mercy will be shown to anyone who has not been merciful. Mercy triumphs over judgment."*

Always pray for discernment and for your fellow believers with all kinds of prayers. If we do as the Holy Bible says, then we are not hearers only, and we will be assured that we are living according to the standards of Christ our Redeemer.

****

I'M SO TIRED OF THIS "CHURCH" STUFF I COULD JUST...

Occasionally while going to church and being involved in ministry at the church, many people become discouraged with "church politics" and with some other people in ministry. This is common among believers, especially when things are not going the way we believe it should or someone is not performing the way we think they should. Do we just stop going to church or leave to join another church? Let's consider this question for a moment. Before we even join any congregation of believers, we should pray to God to lead us where He would have us go to worship Him. In the Old Testament of the Holy Bible, the Lord instructed the Israelites on where to go to worship Him and present their tithes and offerings.

Notice what is said in Deuteronomy 12:8-14 (NIV):

> *"You are not to do as we do here today, everyone doing as they see fit, since you have not yet reached the resting place and the inheritance the LORD your God is giving you. But you will cross the Jordan and settle in the land the LORD your God is giving you as an inheritance, and he will give you rest from all your enemies around you so that you will live in safety. Then to the place the LORD your God will choose as a dwelling for his Name—there you are to bring everything I command you: your burnt offerings and sacrifices, your tithes and special gifts, and all the choice possessions you have vowed to the LORD.*

And there rejoice before the LORD your God—you, your sons and daughters, your male and female servants, and the Levites from your towns who have no allotment or inheritance of their own. Be careful not to sacrifice your burnt offerings anywhere you please. Offer them only at the place the LORD will choose in one of your tribes, and there observe everything I command you."

God told the Israelites to be careful not to sacrifice their burnt offerings anywhere they pleased. Although we do not offer sacrifices anymore since Christ's ultimate sacrifice, we can use this instruction as a guide in determining where we are to worship. We should be prayerful about all things. There are a multitude of churches to choose from, but God knows what we need and where He has His name. The Spirit of the Lord will lead us to where we should worship if we are sensitive to Him. Once we have found the place where God will have us go for worship, this is where we should bring everything He commands us and rejoice before Him.

If things become frustrating where you are worshiping, it is important to know first and foremost the real reason you are at your current place of worship. It is not for people or to please yourself and family; it is where God has led you to go. It is where He wants you to worship before Him and use your gifts and talents. Maybe you are there to bring about a change to a situation that God chose <u>you</u> to change. Maybe you are going through tests in this church to teach you something or to grow you in the Spirit. We should not give up when confronted with tests and trials in the church. Do not move to another church (or ministry) unless the Lord has told you to do so. We must remember that <u>there is no perfect church</u>. We come to church to seek God, not people or ministries. We should be glad to go the Lord's house for what we can <u>give</u> - such as our time, talents, tenth, our praise and worship. We should stay focused on the reason we go to the Lord's house in the first place; and that is to come near to worship. Also, we need fellowship with believers to encourage one another and to build one another up.

The Holy Bible says in Hebrews 10:24-25, *"And let us consider one another to provoke unto love and to good works: not forsaking the assembling of ourselves together, as the manner of some is; but exhorting one another: and so much the more, as ye see the day approaching."*

Another thing to consider when we think another person is not performing as they should or things are not going the way we think it should, is whether we are harboring envy or selfish ambition in our own hearts. Was someone moved to a higher position than you and you think that you should have that position? Is someone getting the recognition you feel you deserve?

Paul, in writing to the church at Corinth in 2 Corinthians 12:20 stated, *"For I fear, lest, when I come, I shall not find you such as I would, and that I shall be found unto you such as ye would not: lest there be debates, envyings, wraths, strifes, backbitings, whisperings, swellings, tumults [disorder]."*

He warns the Galatians of what actions will keep them out of the kingdom of God when he says in Galatians 5:19-21, *"Now the works of the flesh are manifest, which are these; Adultery, fornication, uncleanness, lasciviousness, Idolatry, witchcraft, hatred, variance, emulations, wrath, strife, seditions, heresies, envyings, murders, drunkenness, revellings, and such like: of the which I tell you before, as I have also told you in time past, that they which do such things shall not inherit the kingdom of God."*

When we begin to feel these negative feelings or have negative thoughts towards a person or ministry, we should take a look within ourselves to determine the root of these feelings and thoughts. James 4:1-3 (NIV) states:

> *"What causes fights and quarrels among you? Don't they come from your desires that battle within you? You desire but do not have, so you kill. You covet but you cannot get what you want, so you quarrel and fight. You do not have because you do not ask God. When you ask, you do not receive, because you ask with wrong motives, that you may spend what you get on your pleasures."*

He states further in chapter 3:13-18 (NIV, (emphasis mine):

> *"Who is wise and understanding among you? Let them show it by their good life, by deeds done in the humility that comes from wisdom. But <u>if you harbor bitter envy and selfish ambition in your hearts, do not boast about it or deny the truth</u>. Such "wisdom" does not come down from heaven but is earthly, unspiritual, demonic. For where you have envy and selfish ambition, there you find disorder and every evil practice. But the wisdom that comes from heaven is first of all pure; then peace-loving, considerate, submissive, full of mercy and good fruit, impartial and sincere. Peacemakers who sow in peace reap a harvest of righteousness."*

If you find that you are having thoughts or feelings that are not of God, don't deny them — confess them and pray for forgiveness.

Philippians 2:3-4 states, *"Let nothing be done through strife or vainglory [conceit]; but in lowliness of mind let each esteem other better than themselves. Look not every man on his own things, but every man also on the things of others."*

Do not give up doing what is good. The Lord does see your work and He will reward you in due season. Remember Galatians 6:9, *"Let us not become **weary** in doing good, for at the proper time we will reap a harvest if we do not give up,"* (emphasis mine).

Review previous information on "What happens when I fall?" and "What the Bible says about church."

****

REVIEW

DEALING WITH FELLOW CHRISTIANS/UNBELIEVERS/ENEMIES

1. Discuss your experiences in dealing with your fellow brothers and sisters in Christ:
___
___

2. How have you handled disagreements with a fellow Christian?
___
___

3. Have you ever found yourself condemning someone for their wrong and not talking to them or praying for their restoration and well being? Yes __ No __

4. If yes, did you do anything about the situation according to biblical standards or did you find yourself slipping into gossip?
___
___

5. Describe an occasion when you witnessed to an unbeliever:
___
___

6. Have you ever done something good for a person considered to be an enemy? Explain:
___
___

7. Describe an occasion when you had to make a judgment call using Christian standards:
___
___

8. Discuss some things we can do as Christians to improve our relationship and fellowship in the church environment:
___
___

CHAPTER 8

DEALING WITH SICKNESS, DISEASE AND DEATH
(How could this happen to me? I'm a devoted Christian!)

At one time or another, we all have to deal with sickness, disease, and death. This is a painful time and usually very stressful. We are not at our best when we experience these inevitable times in life. They call for patience, perseverance, wisdom, knowledge, and understanding. They cause us to take a pause from our busy lives and focus on healing — be it physical, mental, or emotional healing. Sometimes we bring sickness on ourselves by what we do to our bodies, but sometimes we experience sickness or disease over which we had no control. Either way, we must deal with the sickness or disease. Many times during these experiences we begin to question why we as Christians must suffer from sickness and disease or go through the pain of losing a loved one (especially if that loved one was a Christian).

Just as the rain falls on the just and the unjust, so sickness, disease, and death come to the just and the unjust. There is one big difference, however, between when the just get sick and when the unjust get sick. That is the just are not forsaken, or utterly cast down (even in death), and we will live again. This is not so with the unjust. They will be destroyed. Let us consider what the Holy Bible says about the righteous and the ungodly in Psalm 1:

> *"Blessed is the man that walketh not in the counsel of the ungodly, nor standeth in the way of sinners, nor sitteth in the seat of the scornful. But his delight is in the law of the LORD; and in his law doth he meditate day and night. And he shall be like a tree planted by the rivers of water, that bringeth forth his fruit in his season; his leaf also shall not wither; and whatsoever he doeth shall prosper."*

"The ungodly are not so: but are like the chaff which the wind driveth away. Therefore the ungodly shall not stand in the judgment, nor sinners in the congregation of the righteous. For the LORD knoweth the way of the righteous: but the way of the ungodly shall perish."

We as Christians know that God's way is not our way and His thoughts are not our thoughts. God knows the end from the beginning. Therefore it is impossible for us to totally understand what God is up to all the time. We can know and trust that everything that happens to His children is for our good, even if we are unable to understand all He is doing.

It is during these times that we must put Proverbs 3:5 into practice which says, *"Trust in the LORD with all thine heart; and lean not unto thine own understanding."* The only thing we need to understand is that God is in control and He knows best what is right and proper in all circumstances.

****

WHEN I OR A LOVED ONE GETS SICK OR SOMEONE DIES, AM I NOT EXERCISING ENOUGH FAITH? IS GOD TRYING TO PUNISH ME?

Faith in all circumstances is good because without it, it is impossible to please God; so yes, exercising faith in this situation is very good. Some people feel that when they do get sick, it is because they have not exercised <u>enough</u> faith or God is punishing them for some sin. This is usually not the case. Sometimes sickness and disease come no matter how strong our faith is. The reason for the sickness could be so you can minister to someone else in the same situation, it may be a trial and test to expose something unconquered in us, it may be so that the glory of God can be revealed, it may be to humble us, or to allow opportunity to seek God's face. There could be a number of reasons for sickness, disease, or death; only God knows why and we have to trust that He knows best and loves best.

When we become Christians, we have no guarantee that we will not suffer. As a matter of fact, suffering is a part of sharing Christ's life. It is written in Romans 8:17 (emphasis mine), *"And if children, then heirs; heirs of God, and joint-heirs with Christ; if so be that we <u>suffer with him</u>, that we may be also glorified together."* Suffering also develops perseverance in us as stated in Romans 5:3 (NIV, emphasis mine), *"Not only so, but we also glory in our sufferings, because <u>we know that suffering produces perseverance.</u>"*

This sounds harsh, but I have realized through my own sufferings that developing patience and perseverance through suffering has made me a stronger person. I am not so overwhelmed when trouble comes. I look back on my last trial and realize that God brought me through that trouble, and He will bring me through this one also.

While I am in the middle of it, I say "God is in control and I will make it through this trial also"; however, I confess that the confidence is not as strong in the middle of it. As I persevere under the trial, my confidence grows and the trial has less power over me.

It hurts going through the trial, and you sometimes feel all alone. Sometimes you wonder, "Lord how long will I have to suffer through this?" Have you ever heard the saying "what doesn't kill you makes you stronger"? I believe the saying is true. Sometimes, we get to a point when we feel we are going to die. But thanks be to God that He is sovereign and knows how much we can bear. He wants to know that we are going to trust Him in these trials. There is another saying that goes, "If you pray, don't worry and if you worry, don't pray." Not worrying is easier said than done. I have learned to say that I am "concerned" about the situation, but God has worked it out.

> I believe a healthy concern is good because it forces us to our knees to seek the Lord about what to do in the situation. There could be something in us, physically or emotionally, that is not conquered and is causing us to be ill. The trial exposes this issue and lets us know what we need to pray about and work on for healing.

1 Corinthians 6:19 - 20 states, *"know ye not that your body is the temple of the Holy Ghost which is in you, which ye have of God, and ye are not your own? For ye are bought with a price: therefore glorify God in your body, and in your spirit, which are God's."* I have learned that I need to take care of the temple the Holy Spirit. If I am not at my best — if I am tired or sick — I am ineffective in work, play, and witness. I have learned to pray to the Lord to show me how to take care of this body in which He dwells. I have started to pay close attention to what foods are good for me and what foods cause bad reactions like indigestion, bloating, headaches, etc. I try to drink plenty of water during the day although I don't want it all the time. Exercise plays a key role in our health, so I try to exercise regularly, even if it is just walking a few miles per week.

I have learned that it is OK to go to doctors (who know generally more than me about the body), heed most of their advice, and learn about my own body. I have learned that I also need to take an active role in my own health, in conjunction with the doctors. I know <u>my</u> body better than they do and I need to share with them what is going on in my body (all the little aches and pains that may be important to their diagnosis).

I have learned that God has already provided us what we need to have a healthy body and we need to pray for discernment on what natural things to do, even if we must sometimes take chemical medications for immediate relief. I must cling to the Lord and allow Him to teach me, and then I must do what He says.

I have learned that life is a school and we never stop learning. I have patience with myself because I make mistakes. As long as I take an active role in learning from my mistakes, rectify them if I can, repent (which means turning away from what I used to practice), judge myself, and be persistent in trying to learn from the Word, I will be more than a conqueror! It takes time, practice, sacrifice, and discipline.

Even in sickness and disease, tests and trials must come so that we may be strong and complete, not lacking anything. These tests increase our faith, knowledge, and wisdom as far as our health is concerned. This too is a part of making an instrument that is strong and ready for work in the Kingdom of God. Do not fret when sickness comes; just know that there is something to learn, something to grow from, or something to conquer. Be patient and learn your lesson about health; relax and pray and take time to grow in the Word. Trust God no matter what happens; say aloud, "Lord I still trust you," whatever the news. Be steadfast and immovable no matter what the doctors say. God will bring you through it and you will live and not die if your work here is not done. He will bring you through to another place if your work is done and you will still live, only on a different plane. Trust God always!

****

CALL FOR THE ELDERS OF THE CHURCH

The Holy Bible also says in James 5:14-15, *"Is any sick among you? let him call for the elders of the church; and let them pray over him, anointing him with oil in the name of the Lord: And the prayer of faith shall save the sick, and the Lord shall raise him up; and if he have committed sins, they shall be forgiven him."* This is not done so much in churches these days, but personally I think it still should be done. I believe when an elder in the church is sometimes hesitant about praying the prayer of faith over the sick, it is because he/she does not want the responsibility when the person does not recover. Some do not believe that healing miracles are for today. Well, when I am sick, I call for the elders of the church. I do this in obedience to the Word. If they pray and I am not healed, I do not say to myself, "His/her faith must not have been strong enough." It is not the elder's responsibility for healing me — it is the Lord's. God is my Jehovah Rapha, the Lord that heals. I give no responsibility (or credit) to man for healing. I honor the elders and appreciate their obedience to the Word. Whether I am healed or not, I feel satisfied that I have been obedient to the Word.

I also consider whether I have unconfessed sin in my life, confess it, repent, and ask for forgiveness. Another thing I have to consider is if there is anything which the Lord has told me to do and I have not been obedient. Am I harboring any sin or thing that is not Christ-like in my heart? These are things that I must pray about and ask for the Lord's help in resolving.

There is also something called intercessory prayer where we pray to God on behalf of someone else. We pray for their healing and well being. Ephesians 6:18 states, *"Praying always with all prayer and supplication in the Spirit, and watching thereunto with all perseverance and supplication for all saints."*

1 Peter 5:6-10 states (emphasis mine), *"Humble yourselves therefore under the mighty hand of God, that he may exalt you in due time: casting all your care upon him; for he careth for you. <u>Be sober, be vigilant; because your adversary the devil, as a roaring lion, walketh about, seeking whom he may devour</u>: whom resist stedfast in the faith, <u>knowing that the same afflictions are accomplished in your brethren that are in the world</u>. But the God of all grace, who hath called us unto his eternal glory by Christ Jesus, after that <u>ye have suffered a while</u>, <u>make you perfect, establish, strengthen, settle you</u>. To him be glory and dominion forever and ever. Amen."*

****

WHEN A RIGHTEOUS MAN DIES

What about the issue of death? Sometimes it seems so unfair when we have prayed for a family member or friend's recovery and they die anyway. It's so sad when a child dies or disaster strikes and we wonder how a loving God could allow this to happen. It shows, once again, that His thoughts are not our thoughts and His ways are not our ways.

> The Holy Bible records in Isaiah 55:9 that, *"For my thoughts are not your thoughts, neither are your ways my ways, saith the LORD. For as the heavens are higher than the earth, so are my ways higher than your ways, and my thoughts than your thoughts."*

I believe the concept of death is different and so much deeper for the Lord than for us as mere mortals. On occasion in the Holy Bible, Jesus refers to someone as not dead, but asleep and says that people who live by believing in Him will never die:

- Mark 5:39 – *"And when he was come in, he saith unto them, Why make ye this ado, and weep? the damsel is not dead, but <u>sleepeth</u>."*
- John 11:11-14 – *"These things said he: and after that he saith unto them, Our friend Lazarus <u>sleepeth</u>; but I go, that I may awake him out of <u>sleep</u>. Then said his disciples, Lord, if he sleep, he shall do well. Howbeit Jesus spake of his death: but they thought that he had spoken of taking of rest in sleep. Then said Jesus unto them plainly, Lazarus is dead."*
- John 11:24-26 - *"Martha saith unto him, I know that he shall rise again in the resurrection at the last day. Jesus said unto her, I am the resurrection, and the life: <u>he that believeth in me, though he were dead, yet shall he live: and whosoever liveth and believeth in me shall never die</u>. Believest thou this?"*

Other verses in the Holy Bible use the word "sleep" for death; and death is explained in a different way:

- Acts 7:59-60 – *"And they stoned Stephen, calling upon God, and saying, Lord Jesus, receive my spirit. And he kneeled down, and cried with a loud voice, Lord, lay not this sin to their charge. And when he had said this, he <u>fell asleep</u>."*
- Acts 13:36 – *"For David, after he had served his own generation by the will of God, <u>fell on sleep</u>, and was laid unto his fathers."*
- 1 Corinthians 11:29-30 – *"For he that eateth and drinketh unworthily, eateth and drinketh damnation to himself, not discerning the Lord's body. For this cause many are weak and sickly among you, and many <u>sleep</u>."*
- 1 Corinthians 15:6 - *After that, he appeared to more than five hundred of the brothers and sisters at the same time, most of whom are still living, though some have <u>fallen asleep.</u>*
- 1 Corinthians 15:17-22 – *"And if Christ be not raised, your faith is vain; ye are yet in your sins. Then they also which are <u>fallen asleep</u> in Christ are perished. If in this life only we have hope in Christ, we are of all men most miserable. But now is Christ risen from the dead, and become the firstfruits of them that <u>slept</u>. For since by man came death, by man came also the resurrection of the dead. For as in Adam all die, even so **in Christ shall all be made alive**."*
- 1 Thessalonians 4:15 – *"For this we say unto you by the word of the Lord, that we which are alive and remain unto the coming of the Lord shall not prevent them which are <u>asleep</u>."*
- 1 Thessalonians 5:10 – *"Who died for us, that, whether we wake or <u>sleep</u>, we should live together with him,"* (emphases mine).

The phrase "fall asleep" softens the word "death." The verses of scripture written above indicate that those who are in Christ fall asleep in Him and will be raised to life again. This makes me feel safe and eases my sorrow when I think of dying or see a loved one who is in Christ die; for I know that we all will sleep and find rest in Him until we are raised again.

When I think of children dying young, I know that they have angels in heaven as written in Matthew 18:9-11 (NIV), *"See that you do not despise one of these little ones. For I tell you that their angels in heaven always see the face of my Father in heaven."*

I know and am confident from scripture that the dead will rise again and no longer die as stated previously and in Luke 20:35-37, *"But they which shall be accounted worthy to obtain that world, and the resurrection from the dead, neither marry, nor are given in marriage: Neither can they die any more: for they are equal unto the angels; and are the children of God, being the children of the resurrection. Now that the dead are raised, even Moses shewed at the bush, when he calleth the Lord the God of Abraham, and the God of Isaac, and the God of Jacob,"* (emphasis mine).

> Per Isaiah 57:1-2 (NIV), *"The righteous perish, and no one takes it to heart; the devout are taken away, and no one understands that the righteous are taken away to be spared from evil. Those who walk uprightly enter into peace; they find rest as they lie in death."*

This is the conclusion of the matter, 1 Corinthians 15:51-58 (NIV):

"Listen, I tell you a mystery: We will not all sleep, but we will all be changed— in a flash, in the twinkling of an eye, at the last trumpet.

For the trumpet will sound, the dead will be raised imperishable, and we will be changed. For the perishable must clothe itself with the imperishable, and the mortal with immortality.

When the perishable has been clothed with the imperishable, and the mortal with immortality, then the saying that is written will come true: 'Death has been swallowed up in victory.' 'Where, O death, is your victory? Where, O death, is your sting?'

The sting of death is sin, and the power of sin is the law. But thanks be to God! He gives us the victory through our Lord Jesus Christ. Therefore, my dear brothers and sisters, stand firm. Let nothing move you.

Always give yourselves fully to the work of the Lord, because you know that your labor in the Lord is not in vain!"

When I consider the above scripture, I find peace.

****

REVIEW

> DEALING WITH SICKNESS, DISEASE, AND DEATH

1. Why should we, as Christians, share in Christ's sufferings?
   _____
   _____
   _____

2. Do you find that you pay more attention to self rather than trusting in God when you are sick? Yes __ No __

3. List a few ways that we as Christians can get through a period of sickness:
   _____
   _____
   _____

4. Why is it important to take care of "The Temple of The Holy Spirit," or our bodies?
   _____
   _____
   _____
   _____

5. What is intercessory prayer?
   _____
   _____
   _____

6. How is death different for a righteous person than for an unrighteous person?
   _____
   _____
   _____

7. Explain the phrase "fall asleep."
   _____
   _____
   _____
   _____

CHAPTER 9

PRESSING TOWARD THE MARK
(If the Salt Loses its Saltiness)

Sometimes in this Christian walk we become tired and discouraged, or we may become prideful. There will be times when we feel that we have worked as hard as we can and we are just not seeing the results manifested as they should be. There will be times when things that we have prayed for and hoped for just do not happen. There will be times when we are distracted and taken off course. There may be times when we allow pride to get in the way of our ministry or put our opinions or the opinions of others above what God has told us to say or do. Sometimes we may feel that we have done everything in vain.

> When these emotions enter into our souls, or when these things happen, we find that we are not as effective as a Christian and we may lose our witness. It may cause us to fall away or forsake our call and, ultimately, Jesus Christ.

I remember times when I felt like my Christian journey was such a struggle. I thought to myself, "You are doing something wrong. It should not be this hard to live right and love others as God loves them." I must confess that I was more comfortable with me and Jesus alone. Yes, just me and Jesus! When it's just us, I do not have to worry about saying something to hurt someone's feelings or make them mad; and they would not hurt mine or make me mad. I do not have to worry about being "nice" or compassionate. I do not have to worry about witnessing to anyone. Jesus and I could just get done what we needed to get done and go home to enjoy a peaceful evening together. Sometimes, however, I would leave Jesus out of my routine. Sometimes, I did not feel like reading the Holy Bible or I could not focus long enough to pray properly. Sometimes I sat and worried about the next day.

When we are at this point, there is something missing in our relationship with Christ. Being with Him should bring peace and joy. If not, we have to check our **love** walk. If our love walk is deficient, we are unable to receive the love we need from God and we are not able to love others properly. When we stray or just have been away from His presence too long, we need to be reinstated, refilled, and refueled for service. We need to first have our hearts right towards Christ to be ready and equipped vessels for the service of others.

We should check our motivation for doing what we do. We should get back in His presence and press our way through our tests and trials; fast, pray, and seek His face even more, despite how we may feel at the time. The devil wants us to be so distracted that we leave the presence of God, and become so frustrated that we give up.

> Sin (whether it is doubt and unbelief, fear, pride, selfishness, etc.) will cause us to be separated from God so that we are not connected as we should be and we become restless wanderers. This is because we have not mastered sin according to Genesis 4:7.

The most Spiritual icons on earth sometimes suffer from what I call "Spiritual Amnesia." We forget who we are in Christ. The symptoms are:

- For want of popularity (or popular opinion), worldly, carnal views seep into sermons and teachings – we crave the good opinion of man
- Pride seeps in causing one to fall away from grace (enticed by sin); humility leaves and self enters
- Fear immobilizes us and we are not able to finish what we were called to do
- Confusion hinders our progress
- Sadness, despondency, irritability, anger, hurt, resentments, rebellion, or depression begins to manifest in our spirits
- The desire for other things distracts us and we do not fulfill our call.

How do we maintain our zeal and devotion to God as Christ's ambassadors? First, we must realize that the devil uses our minds and emotions to trick us and make us think that things are really as they appear. This is not so all the time — things are not always as they appear. The Lord told the Jews in John 7:24 to stop judging by mere appearances and make a right judgment.

While we are here on this earth, we know in part and we understand in part. Paul says in 1 Corinthians 13:12, *"For now we see through a glass, darkly; but then face to face: now I know in part; but then shall I know even as also I am known."* The devil tries to distort our view on heavenly things and the promises of God. He tries to make us think we are not worthy of our call or make us put pride first. He tells us that no one will listen to our "foolishness" or he may say something like, "You can make more money off of this. The crowd loves you!" However, as Christians we are not unaware of his devices.

When the devil goes into action in our minds, we must determine the source of the thought by viewing it in light of scripture (Is the thought true? Is it peace loving? Does it agree with scripture? Is it pure?). If the source of the thought is not the Holy Spirit, cast it down. Say aloud, "I cast that thought down in the name of Jesus!" or, "I rebuke the thought in Jesus' name!" Begin to focus and meditate on what the scripture says about the situation.

> Press through pain and pressure and put your trust in God no matter what you feel, or how the situation may look!

Please read the parable of the sower in Luke 8:4-15.

****

MEET THE PRESS

"Brethren, I count not myself to have apprehended: but this one thing I do, forgetting those things which are behind, and reaching forth unto those things which are before, I press toward the mark for the prize of the high calling of God in Christ Jesus," (Philippians 3:13-14, emphasis mine).

There are certain things in life that you <u>must</u> press through, though it seems impossible to bear. Some are listed as follows:

- <u>Press through trials</u> — produces patience, perseverance, and strength (James 1:2-4)
- <u>Press through sickness and disease</u> – invokes God's grace; encourages discipline in caring for the body (2 Corinthians 12:7-10; 1 Peter 5:10; 1 Corinthians 9:26-27)
- <u>Press through pain and sorrow</u> – Ensures victory and joy on the other side (Psalms 30:5; 1 Peter 2:19)
- <u>Press through fear</u> – Brings confidence when we face and fight fear; builds faith (Exodus 20:20; 2 Timothy 1:7; Jeremiah 1:7-8;17; Psalms 23:4)
- <u>Press through the temptation to give up/give in</u> – Ensures victory; endurance; builds character (1 Corinthians 10:13; James 4:7)

- <u>Press through temptation to sin</u> – learn fight or flight (2 Corinthians 10:3-5; 1 Timothy 1:18; 2 Timothy 2:4; Matthew 10:23; 1 Corinthians 6:18;10:14; 2 Timothy 2:22)
- <u>Press through criticism, pressure, and opposition</u> – develops confidence in the Christ in you in the presence of people and the enemy (Acts 4:13; Jeremiah 1:19; Psalms 23:5; Acts 11:1-18; Acts 4:5-12; Isaiah 54:17; Psalms 27)
- <u>Press through tests and avoid cynicism, grumbling and complaining</u> – Encourages us to put our trust in God and not worry about or judge man (Exodus 20:20; Matthew 9:14-15; Luke 18:10-14; Malachi 3:13-15; Philippians 2:14; 1 Peter 4:9)

When things are not going our way, it is easy to lose focus and motivation to continue. In these times, we must <u>hold fast to the following scriptures:</u>

- Jeremiah 29:11(NIV) – *"For I know the plans I have for you," declares the LORD, "plans to prosper you and not to harm you, plans to give you hope and a future."*
- Isaiah 54:17 – *"No weapon that is formed against thee shall prosper; and every tongue that shall rise against thee in judgment thou shalt condemn. This is the heritage of the servants of the LORD, and their righteousness is of me, saith the LORD."*
- Isaiah 41:10 – *"Fear thou not; for I am with thee: be not dismayed; for I am thy God: I will strengthen thee; yea, I will help thee; yea, I will uphold thee with the right hand of my righteousness."*
- Hebrews 13:5 – *"Let your conversation be without covetousness; and be content with such things as ye have: for he hath said, I will never leave thee, nor forsake thee."*
- Luke 10:19 – *"Behold, I give unto you power to tread on serpents and scorpions, and over all the power of the enemy: and nothing shall by any means hurt you."*
- Philippians 4:6-9 – *"Be careful for nothing; but in everything by prayer and supplication with thanksgiving let your requests be made known unto God. And the peace of God, which passeth all understanding, shall keep your hearts and minds through Christ Jesus.*

Finally, brethren, whatsoever things are true, whatsoever things are honest, whatsoever things are just, whatsoever things are pure, whatsoever things are lovely, whatsoever things are of good report; if there be any virtue, and if there be any praise, think on these things. Those things, which ye have both learned, and received, and heard, and seen in me, do: and the God of peace shall be with you."

- 2 Corinthians 10:3-5 – *"For though we walk in the flesh, we do not war after the flesh: (For the weapons of our warfare are not carnal, but mighty through God to the pulling down of strong holds;) casting down imaginations, and every high thing that exalteth itself against the knowledge of God, and bringing into captivity every thought to the obedience of Christ."*
- 1 John 4:4 – *"Ye are of God, little children, and have overcome them: because greater is he that is in you, than he that is in the world."*
- James 4:7-8 – *"Submit yourselves therefore to God. Resist the devil, and he will flee from you. Draw nigh to God, and he will draw nigh to you."*

Know that all is well and hold on to the Lord for dear life! We must continue and persist in doing the following <u>even when we don't feel like it</u>:

- Be constant in prayer, even if you have to begin to pray short prayers again. Pray in tongues when you cannot think of what to say.
- Be constant in reading the Word, even if you have to begin to read short passages again. Just do not stop.
- Confess any sin in your life. Forgive, if you have not done so. See if there is any area in your life where you have not obeyed God and get in obedience to Him.
- Pray, fast, meditate. Get off to yourself if need be and allow the Lord to revive and refresh you.
- Slowly, but surely, you will get your zeal back and you will remember once again who you are in Christ and become an effective tool for the Kingdom.

Realize that in all we go through, God <u>is</u> sovereign. He knows what is best for all concerned. His ways are not our ways and His thoughts are not our thoughts. Remember 1 Corinthians 10:13 - *"There hath no temptation taken you but such as is common to man: but God is faithful, who will not suffer you to be tempted above that ye are able; but will with the temptation also make a way to escape, that ye may be able to bear it."*

We have a lot to learn about persevering and pressing into the things of God and developing into sharp instruments for Christ. Growing in the Word of God will enable you to do just that, but it takes time (years of practice and application). Not everyone learns at the same rate; we move from one level to the next based on our submission, surrender of self life, knowledge of the Word, application of biblical principles, and patience. We can compare it to being promoted in school; there are certain tests and lessons that must be learned before we grow and develop.

Let us not be counted among those who were not able to endure to the end, but let it be said of us as Paul said in 2 Timothy 4:7-8, *"I have fought a good fight, I have finished my course, I have kept the faith.*

Henceforth there is laid up for me a crown of righteousness, which the Lord, the righteous judge, shall give me at that day: and not to me only, but unto all them also that love his appearing."

Jeremiah 12:5 (NIV) states, *"If you have raced with men on foot and they have worn you out, how can you compete with horses? If you stumble in safe country, how will you manage in the thickets by the Jordan?"*

> Fight with all your might the battle against fear, flesh, self, and unbelief. Don't give in to sin, but learn to strive, survive, and thrive in the Word and in the world.

Evaluate your growth in the Word of God and where you are by reading handout #11 in chapter 11

****

HOLD UP THE LIGHT

Jesus says in Matthew 5:14-16, *"Ye are the light of the world. A city that is set on an hill cannot be hid. Neither do men light a candle, and put it under a bushel, but on a candlestick; and it giveth light unto all that are in the house. Let your light so shine before men, that they may see your good works, and glorify your Father which is in heaven."* He was referring here to His disciples.

He is speaking to those of us who are His body, the church; people who are called by His name, Christians. He is calling for us to come out of the shadows and into the light, to be bold and let the world know who we are and whose we are. He needs us to be a standard of His very character and being.

Let's read more of what the Holy Bible says about light and darkness (emphases mine):

- John 1:4-9 – *"In him was life; and the life was the <u>light</u> of men. And the <u>light</u> shineth in darkness; and the darkness comprehended it not. There was a man sent from God, whose name was John. The same came for a witness, to <u>bear witness of the Light</u>, that all men through him might believe. He was not that Light, but was sent to bear witness of that Light. That was the <u>true Light, which lighteth every man</u> that cometh into the world."*
- John 3:19-21 – *"And this is the condemnation, that <u>light</u> is come into the world, and men loved <u>darkness</u> rather than light, because their deeds were evil. For <u>every one that doeth evil hateth the light</u>, neither cometh to the light, lest his deeds should be reproved. But <u>he that doeth truth cometh to the light</u>, that his deeds may be made manifest, that they are wrought in God."*
- John 8:12 – *"Then spake Jesus again unto them, saying, <u>I am the light of the world</u>: he that followeth me shall not walk in <u>darkness</u>, but shall have <u>the light of life</u>."*
- John 12:36 – *"While ye have light, believe in the light, that ye may be the <u>children of light</u>."*
- John 12:46 – *"I am come a <u>light</u> into the world, that whosoever believeth on me should not abide in <u>darkness</u>."*
- 1 Thessalonians 5:5 – *"Ye are all the children of light, and the children of the day: we are not of the night, nor of darkness."*
- 1 Peter 2:9 – *"But ye are a chosen generation, a royal priesthood, an holy nation, a peculiar people; that ye should shew forth the praises of him who hath <u>called you out of darkness into his marvellous light</u>"*
- 1 John 1:5-7 – *"This then is the message which we have heard of him, and declare unto you, that <u>God is light</u>, and <u>in him is no darkness at all</u>. If we say that we have fellowship with him, and walk in darkness, we lie, and do not the truth. But <u>if we walk in the light, as he is in the light, we have fellowship one with another</u>, and the blood of Jesus Christ his Son cleanseth us from all sin."*
- 1 John 2:9-11 – *"He that saith he is in the light, and hateth his brother, is in darkness even until now. <u>He that loveth his brother abideth in the light</u>, and there is none occasion of stumbling in him. <u>But he that hateth his brother is in darkness</u>, and walketh in darkness, and knoweth not whither he goeth, because that darkness hath blinded his eyes."*

When we accept Christ as our Lord and Savior, we become children of the light because He is light. We should not hide our heritage or act as if we do not know Him or who we are in Him. We are not ashamed of the gospel of Jesus Christ and we are not afraid to share it with the world. When the world looks at us, they see the light of Jesus Christ shining within us and they come near to try to understand this light.

Therein lies our opportunity to share the light with them so they no longer walk in darkness. Displaying our light takes time with the Lord, discipline, diligence in the Word, prayer, fasting, meditation on the Word and love for Christ.

> When we love Christ, and are excited about Him, we want to share Him with the world. We can do this with words, but also without words by letting the world see Him in us, displaying His character and living for Him. In doing this, we are holding up the light for Him and He is pleased with us.

****

KINGDOM PRINCIPLES

We have gone over Christian standards and principles in previous chapters (including chapter 5), so we do not need to go over them again. There is, however, something we need to always keep in mind as we sojourn here on this earth and until Jesus comes, and that is to understand the "principle of the thing," whatever it is. You have heard people say, "It's just the principle of it. I know it's not that bad, can't hurt me or it may be trivial, but it's just the principle of it." What do people mean when they say, "it's just the principle of the thing"?

A *principle* is a standard of conduct. As a Christian believer, in every situation, in making every decision, and in all our planning we must keep in mind "the principle of the thing;" that is, the Kingdom principle. Ask yourself, "What do I stand for?" or "Who do I stand for in this?" The world may think it trivial and not worth considering, but we are always to consider the "Kingdom" principle of the thing. We consider what God's Word says about it, and then we conduct ourselves according to the Kingdom principle or standard.

Some examples are:

1. THE PRINCIPLE OF SOWING AND REAPING

It is indeed a fact that we reap what we sow. Galatians 6:7-8 states *"Be not deceived; God is not mocked: for whatsoever a man soweth, that shall he also reap. For he that soweth to his flesh shall of the flesh reap corruption; but he that soweth to the Spirit shall of the Spirit reap life everlasting."*

2 Corinthians 9:6 states, *"But this I say, He which soweth sparingly shall reap also sparingly; and he which soweth bountifully shall reap also bountifully."*

In life, when we are considering the things that we want, whether it is money, or love, or peace, etc., we should consider the principle of sowing and reaping. The Holy Bible says we reap what we sow; therefore, if I want money, I should sow money. If I want lots of money, I should sow lots of money. If I want love, I should sow love. If I want peace, I should sow peace. It is "the principle of the thing."

2. THE PRINCIPLE OF GIVING

When I sow, I also have to consider the principle of giving which says, *"Give, and it shall be given unto you; good measure, pressed down, and shaken together, and running over, shall men give into your bosom. For with the same measure that ye mete withal it shall be measured to you again,"* (Luke 6:38).

- Give to the poor (Mark 10:21)
- Give what you owe (Romans 13:7)
- Give God a tenth (Luke 11:42)
- Give to widows in need (1 Tim 5:3)
- Give yourself fully to the work of the Lord (1 Corinthians 15:58)

3. THE PRINCIPLE OF SUBMISSION/HUMILITY

The children of God and joint heirs with Christ display Christ's humility. We are not arrogant or prideful. We do not look for praise from men nor do we lift ourselves up. We wait on the Lord and He lifts us up in due time.

James 3:13 states, *"Who is a wise man and endued with knowledge among you? let him shew out of a good conversation his works with meekness of wisdom,"* (emphasis mine).

1 Peter 5:5-6 states, *"Likewise, ye younger, submit yourselves unto the elder. Yea, all of you be subject one to another, and be clothed with humility: for God resisteth the proud, and giveth grace to the humble. Humble yourselves therefore under the mighty hand of God, that he may exalt you in due time,"* (emphasis mine).

Therefore, if I want to be lifted up, I humble myself before God. It's just "the principle of the thing."

4. THE PRINCIPLE OF DENYING SELF

"I am crucified with Christ: nevertheless I live; yet not I, but Christ liveth in me: and the life which I now live in the flesh I live by the faith of the Son of God, who loved me, and gave himself for me," (Galatians 2:20).

Because a Christian is living his/her life for the Lord, instead of for self; we understand that in everything we esteem Him, not self. While it is good to have an excellent self image (which means we know who we are and whose we are in Christ and we perceive the Christ in us), we do not exalt ourselves or esteem ourselves, thereby becoming conceited. Instead of believing in and trusting in ourselves, we believe in and trust in "the Christ in us."

The confidence we have in ourselves is in the Christ within us. We know that He that is within us is greater than our "self" and greater than he that is in the world. Therefore, we are confident <u>in Christ</u>, that we can do all things through Him that strengthens us.

The flesh is the carnal part of a person; it is the physical body or having to do with the unrenewed nature of man. This nature is stubborn and unyielding to the Spirit. It is our "sin nature" or our carnal "self." When we hear people say, "I'm only human," this usually means "I have a fallen nature; I'm not perfect." This statement usually follows some mistake made or damage done to justify the error. While this statement is partly true (we are human in nature), we also have another part of us which is spiritual. The Holy Spirit lives in us and we should follow after the Spirit, not our humanity or flesh.

Jesus told Nicodemus in John 3:5-7, *"Jesus answered, Verily, verily, I say unto thee, except a man be born of water and of the Spirit, he cannot enter into the kingdom of God. That which is born of the flesh is flesh; and that which is born of the Spirit is spirit. Marvel not that I said unto thee, Ye must be born again."*

When we become Christians, we inherit a new nature and are born again, "not of natural descent, of human decision or a husband's will, but born of God," (John 1:13-NIV).

Romans 8:5-14 says:

"For they that are after the flesh do mind the things of the flesh; but they that are after the Spirit the things of the Spirit. For to be carnally minded is death; but to be spiritually minded is life and peace. Because the carnal mind is enmity against God: for it is not subject to the law

of God, neither indeed can be. So then they that are in the flesh cannot please God.

"But ye are not in the flesh, but in the Spirit, if so be that the Spirit of God dwell in you. Now if any man have not the Spirit of Christ, he is none of his. And if Christ be in you, the body is dead because of sin; but the Spirit is life because of righteousness. But if the Spirit of him that raised up Jesus from the dead dwell in you, he that raised up Christ from the dead shall also quicken your mortal bodies by his Spirit that dwelleth in you. Therefore, brethren, we are debtors, not to the flesh, to live after the flesh. For if ye live after the flesh, ye shall die: but if ye through the Spirit do mortify the deeds of the body, ye shall live. For as many as are led by the Spirit of God, they are the sons of God."

Denying self/flesh also means to deny certain pleasures to yourself for the cause of Christ, such as denying yourself food for a time of fasting, or denying yourself television watching time for Word study time, or denying yourself sleep for a time of prayer.

The principle of denying self says, "I will put no confidence in myself and will not follow after my fleshly desires. I will follow after the Spirit of God in all things."

****

RIGHTEOUSNESS, PEACE, AND JOY IN THE HOLY SPIRIT

Per Romans 14:17, *"the kingdom of God is not meat and drink; but righteousness, and peace, and joy in the Holy Ghost."*

The only thing that counts in this Christian walk is faith in Jesus Christ, expressing itself through love for God and man. Once we mature in the faith, we realize this more and more — nothing else matters. We are able to relax and let go of stress and stressors. We realize that most things are just not that serious. God is in control and the world is not; I am not in control. When we release control and allow God to guide our lives, we experience that peace and joy in the Holy Spirit. This takes time, discipline in the Word, prayer, knowledge, wisdom, submission to the Spirit in us, patience, perseverance, and lots of love.

The war between our flesh and spirit will remain, and we will not always be in control of our emotions; sometimes we will fall. The main thing is that we know we are covered by the blood of Jesus and He will supply all our needs according to

His riches in glory. We need to know that if the Lord is truly in us, we will not fall beyond redemption. We can always confess, repent and be cleansed (1 John 1:9).

I have learned to be cheerful when speaking to others, sincere when there is an issue, sympathetic when necessary, strong in my convictions, and always honest and truthful. I try to do everything with purpose and intent, speaking the truth in love and without excuse. I do not claim to be without sin and so deceive myself (1 John 1:8), but when I fall, I confess my sins. I am not perfect, but I try daily to forget those things which are behind me and reach for those things which are before me. I am pressing toward that mark for the prize of my higher calling in Christ Jesus (Phil 3:13).

I have experienced a peace that I have never felt before, even in the midst of turmoil. I may not have all that I long to have, but I have peace. I know that I am the righteousness of Christ, and He is in me and beside me working all things out for my good.

****

FELLOWSHIP WITH GOD

The greatest experience in life is fellowship with God. To have that constant communion with Him is what we should strive for. If anyone has experienced the high that one receives while being "in the Spirit," they know that this high is not comparable with any other high experienced on earth. There is a type of euphoria that cannot be explained. It is not like a drug high; it is not like a sensual, physical high. It is a mystery to me how I am able to feel this joy and ecstasy and peace to overflowing, but God has made provision for His people to have this rapturous feeling when we really commune with Him. I hope that you and every person living will at least once, preferably often, experience this "Holy Ghost High."

The Spirit is a real Gentleman. He will not come unless asked and welcomed in. He is the lover of our souls. It is not like a male-female kind of love; it is more like a love between a Creator and His creation. It is in no way gender based; it is total and complete love, and it is real.

David expressed his love for God in Psalm 18:1-3 (NIV) as follows:

> *"For the director of music. Of David the servant of the LORD. He sang to the LORD the words of this song when the LORD delivered him from the hand of all his enemies and from the hand of Saul. He said:*

I love you, LORD, my strength.

The LORD is my rock, my fortress and my deliverer;
my God is my rock, in whom I take refuge,
my shield and the horn of my salvation, my stronghold.

I called to the LORD, who is worthy of praise,
and I have been saved from my enemies."

If you know someone who is a believer in Christ, ask them about their personal experience with the love of God and fellowship with the Holy Spirit. I am mentioning all three persons (Father, Son, and Holy Ghost/Spirit) because all are a part of the fellowship, and these three separate <u>persons</u> are one. They are separate in persons, but one and the same Spirit. When we join in with their fellowship, it is truly amazing.

1 Corinthians 1:9 states, *"God is faithful, by whom ye were called unto the fellowship of his Son Jesus Christ our Lord."*

You can make a love song about God/ Jesus/The Holy Spirit; in fact, several love songs have already been made by Christian writers and singers.

HERE'S ONE WAY TO HAVE FELLOWSHIP WITH GOD:

- Go back to chapter 3, the section on "The Spiritual." Read again the formula for connecting with the Holy Spirit. Follow these guidelines in emptying yourself of worldly thoughts.
- Focus your attention on the Lord
- Mutter His Word
- Sing a song of praise to the Lord
- Worship Him for all His beauty and power
- Create a poem or love song, just from you to Him. It can be personal and sung or read only by you or you can share it with others. Make melody in your heart to Him.
- Worship Him with other Believers at church, bow before Him and give Him praise.
- Honor the Lord with your whole being
- When you receive His love, return it to Him.

- There are many ways to do it. Let your creative mind flow. If you are unable to think of anything now, I guarantee that if you continue in His Word and meditate on Him, if you seek after Him with all your heart, He will not disappoint. You will have no choice or other desire but to praise Him and love Him.

This Spiritual high is also a benefit of the "Fellowship of Believers." When you experience it, you will know what I mean. Lift those hands, saints! Give glory to God!

> *The grace of the Lord Jesus Christ, and the love of God, and the communion of the Holy Ghost, be with you all. Amen!* (2 Corinthians 13:14).

****

FELLOWHIP WITH OTHER BELIEVERS (AND UNBELIEVERS)

BELIEVERS:

> *" Then Peter said unto them, 'Repent, and be baptized every one of you in the name of Jesus Christ for the remission of sins, and ye shall receive the gift of the Holy Ghost. For the promise is unto you, and to your children, and to all that are afar off, even as many as the Lord our God shall call.' And with many other words did he testify and exhort, saying, 'Save yourselves from this untoward generation.' Then they that gladly received his word were baptized: and the same day there were added unto them about three thousand souls. And they continued stedfastly in the apostles' doctrine and fellowship, and in breaking of bread, and in prayers. And fear came upon every soul: and many wonders and signs were done by the apostles. And all that believed were together, and had all things common"* (Acts 2:38-44).

It is not the Lord's intention that we should be alone. He has provided everything we need for our good and for the good of others. He is pleased when we fellowship with the saints and love one another. The command to love and fellowship with our brothers and sisters in Christ comes with certain admonitions:

For example:

- 1 John 1:6-7 states, *"If we say that we have fellowship with him, and walk in darkness, we lie, and do not the truth: But if we walk in the light, as he is in the light, we have fellowship one with another and the blood of Jesus Christ his Son cleanseth us from all sin,"* (emphasis mine).
- 1 John 4:20-21 states, *"If a man say, I love God, and hateth his brother, he is a liar: for he that loveth not his brother whom he hath seen, how can he love God whom he hath not seen? And this commandment have we from him, That he who loveth God love his brother also,"* (emphasis mine).

When we open ourselves up to receive the love of God and have fellowship with Him, it is easy to love and have fellowship with our brothers and sisters in Christ. We can practice hospitality with our brothers and sisters according to Romans 12:13.

According to Hebrews 13:2, *"Be not forgetful to entertain strangers: for thereby some have entertained angels unawares."* Invite fellow Christians to your home for dinner or coffee after church or suggest going to a movie or bowling one day.

> Being a Christian does not mean we cannot have fun!

There are so many ways we can communicate with each other these days. Call a sister or brother on the phone to talk about your day or share a word (by talk or text) of encouragement. As mentioned in chapter 5, on Love – do something good for someone daily. We should reach outside of our homes by letter, card, call, text, visit, prayer, etc. to our brother or sister in Christ. This practice of spending more time with our Christian family will foster love in our hearts for them.

We as Christians should learn how to have "balance" in our lives. One day, a good friend of mine, LaVerne, and I decided to meet in Asheville, NC to enjoy a weekend of relaxation at the Biltmore Estates. We found out about their "Segway Tour" and decided to try it. The segway is a two wheeled, self balancing, personal transporter used by some policemen, mall security, private individuals, etc. The tour was a lot of fun, and I learned a valuable lesson from the segway. We had to first practice how to mount and balance ourselves on the segway. Once that was accomplished, we were on our way riding through the estate with ease. We used our bodies to stop, turn, and make the segway go fast or slow.

Afterwards, I compared this to our Christian life. We have to steady ourselves and practice balance before we leap into life, then continue balance and poise. We have to make sure our lives are:

- Not all work, and no play
- Not all suffering and no peace
- Not all rain and no sunshine
- Not all sickness and no health
- Not all loneliness and no fellowship

> The Lord has made provision for our enjoyment as well as for our work; for peace in the midst of suffering, for sunshine and flowers and rivers and oceans, for health and prosperity, for fellowship with others. We must learn to **run this race with poise and grace**! God willing, we will do so!

UNBELIEVERS:

We are Christians and belong to the Family of Believers. This does not mean, however, that we should avoid unbelievers. To do that, we would have to leave this earth. We must, in this life, interact with unbelievers all the time. We have a freedom and a responsibility to live a just life before believers and unbelievers.

Listen to what Paul says in the following verses:

1 Corinthians 10:27-33 (NIV, emphasis mine):

> *"If an unbeliever invites you to a meal and you want to go, eat whatever is put before you without raising questions of conscience. But if someone says to you, 'This has been offered in sacrifice,' then do not eat it, both for the sake of the one who told you and for the sake of conscience...So whether you eat or drink or whatever you do, do it all for the glory of God. Do not cause anyone to stumble, whether Jews, Greeks or the church of God— even as I try to please everyone in every way. For I am not seeking my own good but the good of many, <u>so that they may be saved</u>."*

When we hold up the standard of Christ before unbelievers, it is an encouragement for them to become one of us. To do this, we are allowed to be in contact with unbelievers also (as long as they are not considered antichrist per 2 John 1:7-11). We should not, however, allow Christ's principles and standards to be compromised by them or their practices. We should come from among them when their practices are not Christ-like. Our assignment with unbelievers is to love them and influence them to live a life for Christ.

The Bible does say in 2 Corinthians 6:14, *"Be ye not unequally yoked together with unbelievers: for what fellowship hath righteousness with unrighteousness."* This admonition has to do with being "yoked" together with unbelievers (e.g. in marriage). In farming, a yoke is a harness that joins two animals together so that they work together, move together, and have the same assignment. They are in close relationship with each other and have a common purpose. To be in the company of unbelievers does not mean that we have the same assignment or purpose as an unbeliever. We do not yoke together in marriage to unbelievers or go among them to join in with their ungodly activities and purposes; on the contrary, we do it for their good - to try to save some of them through the Holy Spirit of God.

****

WELCOME INTO THE KINGDOM OF GOD

(AM I CONSIDERED A PART OF GOD'S INHERITANCE, OR IS IT JUST ISRAEL/JEWS?)

Who are they who are considered worthy of the Kingdom of God? Is it not His children; His people to whom He gave the right to His inheritance? Some may question whether these people are the Jewish race only because the Bible says Jesus sent his disciples to the lost sheep of Israel and not the Gentiles (non-Jews):

"These twelve Jesus sent forth, and commanded them, saying, Go not into the way of the Gentiles, and into any city of the Samaritans enter ye not: but go rather to the lost sheep of the house of Israel." – Matthew 10:5-6

While it is true that God chose Israel as His people, He always had a plan of salvation for those who were not born into Israel as stated in Isaiah 49:6:

"And he said, It is a light thing that thou shouldest be my servant to raise up the tribes of Jacob, and to restore the preserved of Israel: I will also give thee for a light to the Gentiles, that thou mayest be my salvation unto the end of the earth."

Also, while Jesus did send His disciples to the lost sheep of Israel first, He sent His apostle Paul to the Gentiles as stated in Acts 9:15:

"But the Lord said unto him, Go thy way: for he is a chosen vessel unto me, to bear my name before the Gentiles, and kings, and the children of Israel."

> Paul says in Romans 1:16, *"For I am not ashamed of the gospel of Christ: for it is the power of God unto salvation to everyone that believeth; to the Jew first, and also to the Greek [who were non-Jew]."*

The old covenant was given to Israel. This was the covenant given to Abraham in blood through circumcision in Genesis 17:7-13 (emphasis mine):

> *"And I will establish my covenant between me and thee and thy seed after thee in their generations for an everlasting covenant, to be a God unto thee, and to thy seed after thee. <u>And I will give unto thee and to thy seed after thee, the land wherein thou art a stranger, all the land of Canaan, for an everlasting possession; and I will be their God</u>. And God said unto Abraham, Thou shalt keep my covenant therefore, thou, and thy seed after thee in their generations.*
>
> *This is my covenant, which ye shall keep, between me and you and thy seed after thee<u>; every man child among you shall be circumcised.</u> And ye shall circumcise the flesh of your foreskin; and it shall be a token of the covenant betwixt me and you. And he that is eight days old shall be circumcised among you, every man child in your generations, he that is born in the house, or bought with money of any stranger, which is not of thy seed. He that is born in thy house, and he that is bought with thy money, must needs be circumcised: and my covenant shall be in your flesh for an everlasting covenant."*

The law (written code) was given to the Israelites through a covenant of blood as stated in Exodus 24:3-8. It was not given to the Gentiles:

> *"And Moses came and told the people all the words of the LORD, and all the judgments: and all the people answered with one voice, and said, All the words which the LORD hath said will we do. <u>And Moses wrote all the words of the LORD</u>, and rose up early in the morning, and builded an altar under the hill, and twelve pillars, according to the twelve tribes of Israel... And he took the book of the covenant, and read in the audience of the people: and they said, All that the LORD hath said will we do, and be obedient. And Moses took the blood, and sprinkled it on the people, and said, <u>Behold the blood of the covenant, which the LORD hath made with you concerning all these words,</u>"* (emphasis mine).

The Israelites, however, broke the covenant by not obeying the laws written in the "Book of the Covenant." God was angry with them and sent them into exile from the land of plenty He promised them to other nations. He promised, however, to bring them back <u>and gather others with them</u> as stated in Isaiah 56:8 (emphasis mine):

The Sovereign LORD declares— "The Lord GOD which gathereth the outcasts of Israel saith, yet will I gather <u>others to him, beside those that are gathered unto him</u>."

Paul addresses the Jewish community concerning their boasting about having the law in Romans 2:17-27:

> *"Behold, thou art called a Jew, and restest in the law, and makest thy boast of God, and knowest his will, and approvest the things that are more excellent, being instructed out of the law; and art confident that thou thyself art a guide of the blind, a light of them which are in darkness, An instructor of the foolish, a teacher of babes, which hast the form of knowledge and of the truth in the law. Thou therefore which teachest another, teachest thou not thyself? Thou that preachest a man should not steal, dost thou steal? Thou that sayest a man should not commit adultery, dost thou commit adultery? Thou that abhorrest idols, dost thou commit sacrilege? Thou that meekest thy boast of the law, through breaking the law dishonourest thou God? For the name of God is blasphemed among the Gentiles through you, as it is written. For circumcision verily profiteth, if thou keep the law: but if thou be a breaker of the law, thy circumcision is made uncircumcision.*
>
> *Therefore if the uncircumcision keep the righteousness of the law, shall not his uncircumcision be counted for circumcision? And shall not uncircumcision which is by nature, if it fulfill the law, judge thee, who by the letter and circumcision dost transgress the law?"*

Romans 2:28-29- *"For he is not a Jew, which is one outwardly; neither is that circumcision, which is outward in the flesh: But he is a Jew, which is one inwardly; and circumcision is that of the heart, in the spirit, and not in the letter; whose praise is not of men, but of God."*

Paul explains in Romans 4:6-16:

> *"Even as David also describeth the blessedness of the man, unto whom God imputeth righteousness without works, Saying,*
>
> *'Blessed are they whose iniquities are forgiven, and whose sins are covered. Blessed is the man to whom the Lord will not impute sin.'*
>
> *"Cometh this blessedness then upon the circumcision only, or upon the uncircumcision also? For we say that faith was reckoned to Abraham for righteousness. How was it then reckoned? When he was in circumcision, or in uncircumcision? Not in circumcision, but in uncircumcision…For the promise, that he should be the heir of the world, was not to Abraham, or to his seed, through the law, but through the righteousness of faith. For if they which are of the law be heirs, faith is made void, and the promise made of none effect: Because the law worketh wrath: for where no law is, there is no transgression. Therefore it is of faith, that it might be by grace; to the end the promise might be sure to all the seed; not to that only which is of the law, <u>but to that also which is of the faith of Abraham; who is the father of us all</u>,"* (emphasis mine).

Paul explains in Romans 9:6-8:

> *"Not as though the word of God hath taken none effect. For they are not all Israel, which are of Israel: Neither, because they are the seed of Abraham, are they all children: but, In Isaac shall thy seed be called. That is, they which are the children of the flesh, these are not the children of God: but the children of the promise are counted for the seed."*

This coming together of Jews and Gentiles was not complete until Christ was crucified. This is why the gospel was preached to the Jews first, then to the Gentiles. The apostle to the Gentiles came after the death, burial and resurrection of Christ and this is when the gospel was preached to the Gentiles. Paul explains this in Ephesians 2:11-22 (emphasis mine):

> *"Wherefore remember, that ye being in time past Gentiles in the flesh, who are called Uncircumcision by that which is called the Circumcision in the flesh made by hands; That at that time ye were without Christ, being aliens from the commonwealth of Israel, and strangers from the*

covenants of promise, having no hope, and without God in the world: But now in Christ Jesus ye who sometimes were far off are made nigh by the blood of Christ.

For he is our peace, who hath made both one, and hath broken down the middle wall of partition between us<u>; Having abolished in his flesh the enmity, even the law of commandments contained in ordinances</u>; for to make in himself of twain one new man, so making peace; And that he might reconcile both unto God in one body by the cross, having slain the enmity thereby: And came and preached peace to you which were afar off, and to them that were nigh.

For through him we both have access by one Spirit unto the Father. Now therefore ye are no more strangers and foreigners, but fellow citizens with the saints, and of the household of God; and are built upon the foundation of the apostles and prophets, Jesus Christ himself being the chief corner stone; In whom all the building fitly framed together groweth unto an holy temple in the Lord: In whom ye also are builded together for an habitation of God through the Spirit."

So now, the old covenant law (<u>written code</u>) of the Israelites/Jews is obsolete. The Jews now have a new covenant written not in a book, but written on their hearts as stated in Hebrews 8:8b-10:

"Behold, the days come, saith the Lord, when I will make a new covenant with the house of Israel and with the house of Judah: Not according to the covenant that I made with their fathers in the day when I took them by the hand to lead them out of the land of Egypt; because they continued not in my covenant, and I regarded them not, saith the Lord.

For this is the covenant that I will make with the house of Israel after those days, saith the Lord; I will put my laws into their mind, and write them in their hearts: and I will be to them a God, and they shall be to me a people."

GENTILES ARE A LAW UNTO THEMSELVES

The Gentiles, who had no law or written code, now too have the law written on their hearts as is written in Romans 2:13-16 (emphasis mine):

> *"For as many as have sinned without law shall also perish without law: and as many as have sinned in the law shall be judged by the law; (For not the hearers of the law are just before God, but the doers of the law shall be justified. <u>For when the Gentiles, which have not the law, do by nature the things contained in the law, these, having not the law, are a law unto themselves: Which shew the work of the law written in their hearts, their conscience also bearing witness, and their thoughts the mean while accusing or else excusing one another;</u>) In the day when God shall judge the secrets of men by Jesus Christ according to my gospel."*

Romans 9:30-32 states:

> *"What shall we say then? That the Gentiles, which followed not after righteousness, have attained to righteousness, even the righteousness which is of faith. But Israel, which followed after the law of righteousness, hath not attained to the law of righteousness. Wherefore? Because they sought it not by faith, but as it were by the works of the law. For they stumbled at that stumbling stone."*

Paul also says in Romans 3:21-26:

> *"But now the righteousness of God without the law is manifested, being witnessed by the law and the prophets; Even the righteousness of God which is by faith of Jesus Christ unto all and upon all them that believe: for there is no difference: For all have sinned, and come short of the glory of God; Being justified freely by his grace through the redemption that is in Christ Jesus: Whom God hath set forth to be a propitiation through faith in his blood, to declare his righteousness for the remission of sins that are past, through the forbearance of God; To declare, I say, at this time his righteousness: that he might be just, and the justifier of him which believeth in Jesus."*

Romans 8:12-17 states:

> *"Therefore, brethren, we are debtors, not to the flesh, to live after the flesh. For if ye live after the flesh, ye shall die: but if ye through the Spirit do mortify the deeds of the body, ye shall live. For as many as are led by the Spirit of God, they are the sons of God. For ye have*

not received the spirit of bondage again to fear; but ye have received the Spirit of adoption, whereby we cry, Abba, Father. The Spirit itself beareth witness with our spirit, that we are the children of God: And if children, then heirs; heirs of God, and joint-heirs with Christ; if so be that we suffer with him, that we may be also glorified together."

> We should <u>become</u> Disciples of Christ, and then we should <u>make</u> disciples of all nations.

STAND FIRM TO THE END!

It seems it has been a long time since Jesus ascended into heaven and some may wonder when or if He will return. But we must hold out and endure to the end.

1 Corinthians 1:8 (NIV) states – *"He will also keep you firm to the end, so that you will be blameless on the day of our Lord Jesus Christ."*

Peter says in 2 Peter 3:3-7:

"Knowing this first, that there shall come in the last days scoffers, walking after their own lusts, and saying, Where is the promise of his coming? For since the fathers fell asleep, all things continue as they were from the beginning of the creation. For this they willingly are ignorant of, that by the word of God the heavens were of old, and the earth standing out of the water and in the water: Whereby the world that then was, being overflowed with water, perished: But the heavens and the earth, which are now, by the same word are kept in store, reserved unto fire against the day of judgment and perdition of ungodly men. But, beloved, be not ignorant of this one thing, that one day is with the Lord as a thousand years, and a thousand years as one day."

He goes on to say in verses 10-14:

"But the day of the Lord will come as a thief in the night; in the which the heavens shall pass away with a great noise, and the elements shall melt with fervent heat, the earth also and the works that are therein shall be burned up. Seeing then that all these things shall be dissolved, what manner of persons ought ye to be in all holy conversation and godliness, Looking for and hasting unto the coming of the day of God,

wherein the heavens being on fire shall be dissolved, and the elements shall melt with fervent heat? Nevertheless we, according to his promise, look for new heavens and a new earth, wherein dwelleth righteousness. Wherefore, beloved, seeing that ye look for such things, be diligent that ye may be found of him in peace, without spot, and blameless."

We want to be able to stand before the Lord in the Day of Judgment and hear him say that we are welcome into His glory.

> Matthew 25:21 - *"His lord said unto him, well done, thou good and faithful servant: thou hast been faithful over a few things, I will make thee ruler over many things: enter thou into the joy of thy lord."*

I'm not suggesting that this walk is easy or that no suffering will be experienced. I am suggesting, however, that in the end, it will be well worth it. Paul says in Romans 8:18, *"For I reckon that the sufferings of this present time are not worthy to be compared with the glory which shall be revealed in us."*

All who have decided to be a part of the "Fellowship of the Believers" and the "Body of Christ,"

WELCOME INTO THE KINGDOM OF GOD!!

****

The Standards of Christian Conduct

REVIEW

PRESSING TOWARD THE MARK

1. Describe a time in your Christian walk when you became discouraged and what you did about it:
_____

2. List ways in which you choose, or will choose to hold up the light for Christ:
_____

3. Describe a Kingdom principle, not listed in this chapter already, and tell how we are to apply it in our lives as Christians:
_____

4. What are some ways we can enjoy righteousness, peace and joy in the Holy Spirit?
_____

5. List ways in which we can have fellowship with God:
_____

6. List ways in which you have or will have fellowship with fellow believers:
_____
_____

7. List way in which you have or will have fellowship with unbelievers:
_____
_____

8. List ways you have learned to balance you life:
_____
_____

9. What is your understanding of Abraham's offspring (Romans 4:13-16; 9:6-8)?
_____
_____

CHAPTER 10

EPILOGUE
(BE A WITNESS)

Now that you have received instruction on Christian living, please, I implore you, walk in your calling and hold up the standard of Christ. As you press into the things of God, you will go from glory to glory to glory. It is not easy, but it is worth it. There is a saying that nothing worth having is easy, but I believe if you persevere in this life, you will reap rewards that you cannot dream of. Today many people claim to be Christians, but it is not proven by the life that they live. Some waver back and forth between being righteous and being worldly. They are what the Holy Bible considers "lukewarm." Revelations 3:16 states, *"So then because thou art lukewarm, and neither cold nor hot, I will spew thee out of my mouth."*

> I challenge you to be different from what you see in the world. Be a light to the believers as well as non-believers. Against all odds, be true to who you are in Christ so that you will be blameless at the end and honored by Christ.

No, you are not perfect and you will make mistakes; but as long as you confess, repent, and learn from your mistakes, you will have victory because Christ is our redeemer and he is our intercessor. *"He that saith, I know him, and keepeth not his commandments, is a liar, and the truth is not in him,"* (1 John 2:4). No one who lives in him keeps on sinning. *"No one who continues to sin has either seen him or known him,"* (1John 3:6, NIV).

Do not allow temptation or your peers or the world to destroy your witness. Be a strong and true witness to the world of the Christ in you. Do not be ashamed of the gospel of Christ, but be bold before the world. When you get weak, go to Jesus Christ for strength and help. You may have to labor before Him for a while, but do not give up.

Philippians 1:27 (NIV, emphasis mine) says *"Whatever happens, <u>conduct</u> yourselves in a manner worthy of the gospel of Christ."*

Jeremiah 17:10 states (NIV, emphasis mine), *"I the LORD search the heart and examine the mind, to reward each person according to their <u>conduct</u>, according to what their deeds deserve."*

He sees you and He loves you. He wants to know that you are serious about Him. He will save you! Never stop trusting and believing in Him.

PERSEVERE IN HIS LOVE, YOU WILL CONQUER! WELCOME TO THE FAMILY OF BELIEVERS!

****

TRUE CONFESSIONS

I have reserved this section of the manual for testimonies and true confessions of people who have actually experienced the power of God and have had His Word work for them in their personal lives. I hope it blesses you and encourages you to persevere in His love. I will start with myself. I am not able to list all, as I have many testimonies, but I will share a few.

My testimony –

1:
I was born with an incurable blood disease. This disease has the capacity to debilitate me and cause me to live a life of permanent disability. It causes excruciating pain when what is called a "crisis" is experienced. You can do nothing but writhe in pain. The pain crisis may last anywhere from a few hours to a few months. Many people diagnosed with this disease are not able to work. There are different forms of the disease that range from less severe to most severe. The type of disease I was diagnosed with is considered one of the most severe. I struggle with telling this testimony because many people who know me do not know that I have a disease. They will find out for the first time while reading this book. I have not shared it with many people because I did not want to be treated any differently than anyone else. People have a way of trying to protect you, not realizing that they are hurting you instead. They say things like, "Oh you better not do this," "I don't think you should try that," or "Don't you think you should sit down?" I decided that in order to have some sem-

blance of a normal life, I would withhold this piece of information from people that I met. I did share this information, later in life, with a few people. I now realize that people need to know my story and maybe it will encourage and help someone who thinks that they have no hope. Maybe it can minister to someone who is hurting and needs to know that he is not alone.

Although I have suffered greatly because of the disease and have had many hospitalizations, I have lived a fairly normal life. I feel like Paul when he says in 2 Corinthians 12:7-10 (NIV):

> *To keep me from becoming conceited because of these surpassingly great revelations, there was given me a thorn in my flesh, a messenger of Satan, to torment me. Three times I pleaded with the Lord to take it away from me. But he said to me, 'My grace is sufficient for you, for my power is made perfect in weakness.' Therefore I will boast all the more gladly about my weaknesses, so that Christ's power may rest on me. That is why, for Christ's sake, I delight in weaknesses, in insults, in hardships, in persecutions, in difficulties. For when I am weak, then I am strong.*

Because God is my strong deliverer, He has allowed me to have few hospitalizations in my latter years, limited crises, and I have felt good most of my life. My family has been a strong support for me. They never treated me as if I had a disease, except for being there for me when I was sick. I praise God for that and I thank my family for being there for me. My mother, Mother Rosa P. Duncan, has been at my side through it all and I thank God for her. She is a strong woman who raised her children basically on her own. What a powerhouse! I will always love and admire her.

I have been blessed to have gone through 12 years of school, 4 years of college, 32 years of work for the federal government, and now I am retired and devoting the rest of my life to living and promoting Christian standards. I have traveled to places like Jamaica, Mexico, Portugal, Honduras, the Bahamas, Aruba, New York, California, Florida, and many other places. God blessed me in ways that I can't begin to explain. No one will ever be able to tell me that it was not God who brought me through (and to) all this. He is the lover of my soul and I love Him and will dwell in Him forever. God is a sustainer!

2:

In September of 2005, I endeavored to sell a townhouse I owned because the neighborhood had declined and it was time to move if I expected to have some equity in the home. I enlisted the help of a friend who was a mortgage broker to sell the house. I was told by him and other neighbors that the house was not going to sell unless I sold it below the market value. The neighborhood had gone down tremendously. I prayed about it, got rid of this mortgage broker, and got a member of my church to help me. She would pray with me and she worked diligently to sell the townhouse. She listed it for more than what the market value was at the time. The house sold within a month and I received $7,000 more than the original listing price. God is real and He is good! He is my source!

3:

In June of 2006, I was involved in a one-car accident in which I lost control of my car on the expressway; it went airborne and landed in the median. The car was totaled. I walked away with a small fracture of my left finger that I was not aware of. It did not hurt, but just felt "funny." The emergency room doctor did an X-ray as a precaution and found out about the fracture. Other than that, I was fine — not another scratch. When I went to claim my car, I could not believe the damage. God truly kept me in that situation. I felt as if an angel of the Lord picked the car up and sat it down in the median. The damage came, I believe, from when the car went between two guard rails. God is a protector!

4:

In January of 2011, I was diagnosed with breast cancer. It was stage "0" cancer that was discovered during a routine mammogram. The cancer had not spread to my lymph nodes, so I did not have to have chemotherapy; I did not have to have radiation therapy; I did not need to go on any drugs for any adjunct treatment. Right now, the doctors say that I am cancer free, PRAISE THE LORD! God is a Healer!

I believe this trial came in order to get me to do what God had been telling me to do all along. I had said that I would retire early many times, but I thought maybe I could continue to work until I reached the required retirement age of 55. That was my plan, but it was not God's plan. He needed me to retire now. There were several indications and messages I received to confirm this. So in March of this year, my employer made an "Early Out" announcement.

With this early out opportunity, I could retire early, receive a reduced pension (reduction was only 2% in my case), receive benefits such as health insurance, life insurance, and a thrift savings plan. I could retire now and focus my attention on what God had for me to do. I know they say the economy is very bad, but I can't tell that it is. Because of the bad economy, my mortgage has dropped $400 per month. God is a provider!

D. Duncan

****

In the fall of 2007, I was blessed to take a 2-year sabbatical to write a book that God placed in my heart. He called me to trust Him by pursuing my writing and starting my own business during one of the most challenging economic times in U.S. history. Once I obeyed Him and stepped out on faith to pursue His purpose and plan for my life, I was blessed with four publishing contracts as well as mentors, resources, and clients. While the economy faltered, I prospered both personally and professionally. This was only due to the grace and favor of God. God has His own agenda for calling us to accomplish extraordinary goals (Ephesians 3:20) that can only be accomplished by Him working through us. We are simply the vehicles.

- Dr. K. Shelette Stewart
  Author, "Revelations in Business: Connecting Your Business Plan with God's Purpose and Plan for Your Life"
  Principal, Stewart Consulting, LLC (www.stewartconsultingLLC.org)
  Associate Director - Executive Education
  Southern Methodist University - Cox School of Business

****

What a MIGHTY GOD we serve. The following is just one of many testimonials I could give of God's goodness and faithfulness in my life:

In June, 2011, my daughter was 23 weeks pregnant with my first grandchild. She developed a condition called "premature shortened cervix." The doctors told us that with her cervix being so short, premature delivery within 2 weeks was highly probable. My daughter was immediately placed in the hospital on full bed rest. If she delivered the baby this early, there would be all kinds of health issues, even if the baby survived. My daughter was filled with fear and very distraught. I told her that the doctors had their say, but I was going to believe God for a term delivery and an excellent outcome for her and the baby and I wanted her to do the same.

She was in and out of the hospital at various times. The doctors seemed baffled that her cervix was so short but she wasn't going into premature labor. The high risk doctors told us was that 37 weeks was the magic number. This would be considered a term delivery for a person with this condition. Each day, I told God that I believed Him for a term delivery and excellent outcome for my daughter and grandchild. I asked my family and friends to pray this prayer with me. On Monday, August 29, 2011 at 3:30PM, my daughter went into labor. The next day she would be 37 weeks pregnant. The nurses told my daughter that they felt sure that the baby would be born before midnight. I told my daughter that the baby would not be born before 12:01 AM on August 30th. I am happy to report that my granddaughter was born at 2:05AM on August 30, 2011 at 37 weeks and in excellent health. My daughter came through just fine. To God be the glory for all the things he has done.

Linda Darrington

****

God has truly been good to me. My husband was diagnosed with colon cancer in 1991. He went through surgery, chemotherapy, and radiation treatment. He went into remission that lasted for 5 years. During this period, he continued to work, was actively involved in his church, and spent time with his family and friends as though nothing was wrong. I would watch him minister to others whom he felt were worse off than he was. The church members did not know that he was sick; neither did my coworkers. I refused to share with anyone because I knew I had to fight this battle alone.

I meditated on God's Word day and night that my husband would be totally healed. The cancer returned in 12/1996. My husband took one dose of chemo treatment and refused to take more because it made him sick. We knew that God is an awesome God and he would not put any more on us than what we could bear. We stood firmly on the Word —Jesus healed them all. In September 1997 when the doctor told me that my husband's time left in his condition was no more than a year, and could be as little as six months, I almost broke down in tears.

I was able to stand in the midst of the storm and I know God gave me the strength to endure.

Lenora Massey

Note: Lenora has persevered under this trial and, because of her faithfulness to God, she has since received a promotion on her job, first to team leader (supervisor), and she is now serving as a Branch Chief.

The Standards of Christian Conduct

****

1:

One Friday night, a few years ago, my children and I were traveling home after a game where my daughter played in Marietta. My son and daughter wanted to spend the night out with some of their friends. I said no, and stuck to my word. They both were mad and pouting, but I stuck to my initial decision. I was traveling on I-285 at about 70 mph heading home when my tire had a blowout. I was in the far left lane headed for the emergency lane closest to me. My son was thinking fast to tell me, "No Mom, get over to the far right." Before I stopped rolling, the Holy Spirit held up the traffic long enough for me to change about four lanes, and I was able to get to the right side of the highway. Thank God for my son thinking clearly enough to make me go to the safest side. I made several calls for help. I called one of my sisters who had AAA and she came to help me. She called AAA and they informed her that the wrecker should arrive within the next <u>hour</u>! I began to panic because the traffic was so heavy. It was late Friday night and I was afraid of how reckless people were driving. I was thinking of some drunken person losing control and hitting us because we were in a dangerous location; it was not well lit. My son turned on the radio to drown out the sound of the passing cars and trucks. I immediately turned it off and told my children that we needed to pray. After we prayed, a few minutes later, a man in a Navigator traveling in the fast lane spotted us and slowed down. He made his way across the highway to the far right lane and backed up until he was right in front of me. He gave me his business card. He said that he would have us rolling in no time at all, and he did. The Lord sent an angel to rescue me and my children. I began to thank the Lord for sending someone so quickly. This is only one of the many testimonies.

2:

There was so much going on in the month of May, 2011. Jayla, who is my youngest niece, had a birthday party for her 11th birthday. There was a nice crowd of people, young and old. The weather was good and the food was excellent. Jayla played hard and even had several girls to stay over. While Jayla was outside jumping on her trampoline, she fell off and must have hurt herself. She was having so much fun that day, she didn't tell her mom that she was hurt. During the next few days Jayla began to act strangely; one of her friends told her mom that something was wrong with Jayla. She was not walking or speaking properly. When her mom became aware of her actions, she called 911 to rush her to Egleston Hospital. This was the beginning of a very difficult time in our lives. I never saw my sister breakdown and cry, but I heard from a friend that she did; I even broke down at work. I knew that God wouldn't put more on me than I could bear.

I watched my niece transition from not talking and walking to learning to do these simple things all over again. I made several trips to the hospital to pray for Jayla and to lay hands on her, anointing her with oil. The first sign was evident when I prayed out loud once. She would close her little eyes and when I finished praying, she would say, "Amen." I knew by her sound & clarity she was on the road to recovery. After the second prayer, she sat up in the bed to play a game with some of her friends. At that time the doctor still didn't know exactly what was going on with her, and was still running tests to find something. This whole dilemma was a mystery. I began praying and fasting for her healing.

We prayed for God to lead us to a doctor who could give us answers about what really happened. They transferred Jayla to Scottish Rite Hospital. The next doctor we met stated that he wanted to get to the root cause of this condition. His conversation with us comforted the family. They tried antibiotics and several different therapies. After several sessions, her motor skills began to improve. My daughter sent a video on her cell phone of Jayla trying to throw a ball. It was a miracle. It almost brought tears to my eyes. My mom could not believe her eyes, but we both witnessed it. One night, I wanted Jayla to pray and she pointed to me for me to pray like I usually would. I really wanted her to pray. I told her that it didn't have to be a long prayer. She closed her eyes and said, "Jesus heal me, Amen." I begin to share with her that the Lord hears our prayers, especially the ones from children. I began to pray; after I finished, I shared with her that the Lord wanted to use her and this would be her testimony. I asked her if she believed and she said in a whisper, "I believe." I saw evidence of her wanting to hear all that God was telling her; she would turn off the TV before I would pray so there wouldn't be any distractions. The enemy tried to attack us many times, but we had to take authority — the devil is a liar. We kept praying in spite of negative words and actions, and we were both victorious. Jayla was hospitalized for a little over a month. I really wish that I had been journaling all activities when they were fresh in my mind. To make a long story short, we witnessed a miraculous healing for Jayla, and her faith was commendable. She is once again the vibrant child we knew and loved! God is awesome! To God Be the Glory!

Charlene Famble

****

Chapter 11

Appendix

LIST OF HANDOUTS:

Handout # 1 - Evaluating My Own Belief System

Handout # 2 - What the Bible Says About Me/Church/Preachers

Handout # 3 - Putting Off the Old Self

Handout # 4 - Putting on the New Self

Handout # 5 - Jesus Trivia Challenge

Handout # 6 - Understanding the Mind

Handout # 7 - Self Inventory

Handout # 8 - Character Evaluation

Handout # 9 - Affirmations

Handout # 10 - Self Evaluation of Mercy and Humility

Handout #11 – Growing in the Word

HANDOUT # 1 – EVALUATING MY OWN BELIEF SYSTEM

(Be honest with yourself about how you really feel)

BELIEF	DO YOU AGREE? Y/N/ M(maybe)	POINTS
Church people are all hypocrites		
Preachers are out to get your money		
Most White people are sneaky and get away with lawbreaking		
Black people are, for the most part, lazy		
Foreigners are taking over "our" country		
Baptists are not saved and/or sanctified		
Jehovah's Witnesses don't really understand the Bible		
I am dumb and stupid. I will never make it in life		
I know more than most people and I can't understand why people act the way they do		
I just cannot get past my pain and suffering!		
God is not fair and does not love me		
You really don't need Jesus to get into The Kingdom of Heaven, all you need to do is be a good person		
Wicked people always get ahead; good people always suffer		
TOTAL POINTS/SCORE	--------------	

Give yourself 2 points for all "Y" answers and 4 points for "N".
Give yourself 3 points for "M" – "I believe this to a certain extent."

If your score is 28-38, you have much work to do on "renewing your mind" into Kingdom thinking. Continue to read the Word and pray for the Lord to reveal the truth about you, other people, and His Kingdom. Research what the Bible says about judging and about love.

If your score is 39-47, you still have some work to do in "renewing your mind" into Kingdom thinking, but you are close to developing a good attitude. Continue to read the Word and pray for the Lord to reveal His wisdom and truth. Research what the Bible says about judging and about love.

If you have a score of 48-56, your mind is not entirely marred by worldly or harmful views. You have, for the most part, a good positive attitude. Continue to pray about any negative attitudes about yourself or other people.

```
28                          42                          56
|------------------|------------------|
Negative,           Middle of the road           Good,
Judgmental          Neither hot nor cold         positive
Attitude                                         attitude
```

SCRIPTURES TO HELP RENEW OUR THINKING

I. <u>The Basics (Taken from the NIV)</u>

   A. God is Fair:

      1. "God is just: He will pay back trouble to those who trouble you." 2 Thessalonians 1:6
      2. "Yet the LORD longs to be gracious to you; he rises to show you compassion. **For the LORD is a God of justice**. Blessed are all who wait for him!" – Isaiah 30:18

   B. What the Holy Bible says about our minds/unity:

      1. "Do not conform any longer to the pattern of this world [or worldly thinking], but be transformed by the renewing of your **mind**. Then you will be able to test and approve what God's will is—his good, pleasing and perfect will." – Romans 12:2
      2. "Those who live according to the sinful nature have their **minds** set on what that nature desires; but those who live in accordance with the Spirit have their **minds** set on what the Spirit desires." – Romans 8:5
      3. "May the God who gives endurance and encouragement give you a spirit of **unity** among yourselves as you follow Christ Jesus."– Romans 15:5
      4. "Set your **mind**s on things above, not on earthly things." – Colossians 3:2

   C. On Judging Others:

1. "Therefore let us stop **passing judgment** on one another. Instead, make up your mind not to put any stumbling block or obstacle in your brother's way." – Romans 14:13
2. "Do not **judge** or you too will be **judged**. For in the same way you **judge** others, you will be **judged**, and with the measure you use, it will be measured to you. Why do you look at the speck of sawdust in your brother's eye and pay no attention to the plank in your own eye?" Matthew 7:1-3
3. "Do not **judge** and you will not be judged. Do not condemn, and you will not be condemned. Forgive, and you will be forgiven." – Luke 6:37

D. On Pride/Humility:

1. "God opposes the proud but shows favor to the humble." – James 4:6

E. On Getting into Heaven:

1. "Jesus answered, 'I am the way and the truth and the life. No one comes to the Father except through me' - John 14:6

HANDOUT #2 - WHAT THE BIBLE SAYS ABOUT ME (NIV)

I Peter 2:9-10 – *But you are a chosen people, a royal priesthood, a holy nation, a people belonging to God, that you may declare the praises of him who called you out of darkness into his wonderful light. Once you were not a people, but now you are the people of God; once you had not received mercy, but now you have received mercy.*

Isaiah 54:17 – *No weapon forged against you will prevail, and you will refute every tongue that accuses you. This is the heritage of the servants of the Lord, and this is their vindication from me, declares the Lord.*

Romans 8:38-39 – *For I am convinced that neither death nor life, neither angels nor demons, neither the present nor the future, nor any powers, neither height nor depth, nor anything else in all creation, will be able to separate us from the love of God that is in Christ Jesus our Lord.*

Luke 10:19 - *I have given you authority to trample on snakes and scorpions and to overcome all the power of the enemy; nothing will harm you.*

2 Corinthians 5:17-18 - *Therefore, if anyone is in Christ, he is a new creation; the old has gone, the new has come! All this is from God, who reconciled us to himself through Christ and gave us the ministry of reconciliation.*

Ephesians 3:16-19 - *I pray that out of his glorious riches he may strengthen you with power through his Spirit in your inner being, so that Christ may dwell in your hearts through faith. And I pray that you, being rooted and established in love, may have power, together with all the saints, to grasp how wide and long and high and deep is the love of Christ, and to know this love that surpasses knowledge—that you may be filled to the measure of all the fullness of God.*

2 Peter 1:4 - *Through these he has given us his very great and precious promises, so that through them you may participate in the divine nature and escape the corruption in the world caused by evil desires.*

WHAT THE BIBLE SAYS ABOUT CHURCH (NKJV)

Matthew 16:18 - *... and on this rock I will build My church, and the gates of Hades [Hell] shall not prevail against it.*

Acts 11:26 - *And when he had found him, he brought him to Antioch. So it was that for a whole year they assembled with the church and taught a great many people. And the disciples were first called Christians in Antioch.*

Acts 14:23 - *So when they had appointed elders in every church, and prayed with fasting, they commended them to the Lord in whom they had believed.*

1 Corinthians 14:12 – *Even so you, since you are zealous for spiritual gifts, let it be for the edification of the church that you seek to excel.*

Ephesians 1:22 - *And He [God] put all things under His [Jesus'] feet, and gave Him to be head over all things to the church.*

Ephesians 3:10 - *... now the manifold wisdom of God might be made known by the church to the principalities and powers in the heavenly places according to the eternal purpose which He accomplished in Christ Jesus our Lord.*

Ephesians 5:23 – *For the husband is head of the wife, as also Christ is head of the church; and He is the Savior of the body.*

Ephesians 5:25 – *Husbands, love your wives, just as Christ also loved the church and gave Himself for her.*

WHAT THE BIBLE SAYS ABOUT PREACHERS (NIV)

1 Timothy 3:1 – *Here is a trustworthy saying: If anyone sets his heart on being an overseer, he desires a noble task. Now the overseer must be above reproach, the husband of but one wife, temperate, self-controlled, respectable, hospitable, able to teach, not given to drunkenness, not violent but gentle, not quarrelsome, not a lover of money. He must manage his own family well and see that his children obey him with proper respect (If anyone does not know how to manage his own family, how can he take care of God's church?). He must not be a recent convert, or he may become conceited and fall under the same judgment as the devil.*

1 Timothy 5:17 – *The Elders who direct the affairs of the church well are worthy of double honor, especially those whose work is preaching and teaching. 5:19 – Do not entertain an accusation against an elder unless it is brought by two or three witnesses.*

Titus 1:7-9 – *Since an overseer is entrusted with God's work, he must be blameless—not overbearing, not quick-tempered, not given to drunkenness, not violent, not pursuing dishonest gain. Rather he must be hospitable, one who loves what is good, who is self-controlled, upright, holy and disciplined. He must hold firmly to the trustworthy message as it has been taught, so that he can encourage others by sound doctrine and refute those who oppose it.*

Acts 20:28 – *Keep watch over yourselves and all the flock of which the Holy Spirit has made you overseers. Be good shepherds of the church of God, which he bought with his own blood.*

1 Corinthians 9:13-14 – *Don't you know that those who work in the temple get their food from the temple, and those who serve at the altar share in what is offered on the altar? In the same way, the Lord has commanded that those who preach the gospel should receive their living from the gospel.*

HANDOUT # 3 - PUTTING OFF THE OLD SELF

Ephesians 4 and 5

IN OUR OLD SELF WE:

- ➢ Were dead in our transgressions and sins
- ➢ Followed the ways of this world and the ruler of the kingdom of the air
- ➢ Gratified the cravings of our sinful nature
- ➢ Were darkened in our understanding and separate from God
- ➢ Were given over to sensuality and indulging in every kind of impurity with a continual lust for more
- ➢ Lived in the futility of our thinking

AS CHILDREN OF THE LIGHT WE:

- ➢ Put off falsehood and speak truthfully to our neighbors
- ➢ Do not sin in our anger or let the sun go down while we are still angry
- ➢ Do not let any unwholesome talk come out of our mouths but only what is helpful in building others up
- ➢ Get rid of all bitterness, rage, anger, brawling, slander, and every form of malice
- ➢ Do not allow a hint of sexual immorality, impurity or greed
- ➢ Do not allow obscenity, foolish talk, or coarse joking
- ➢ Have nothing to do with the fruitless deeds of darkness
- ➢ Put aside the deeds of darkness and put on the armor of light (Rom. 13:12)

HANDOUT # 4 - PUTTING ON THE NEW SELF CREATED TO BE LIKE GOD

Ephesians 5 and 6

- ➢ Our new self is in accordance with the truth that is in Christ Jesus
- ➢ God raised us up with Christ and seated us with Him in heavenly realms in Christ Jesus
- ➢ We are imitators of God as dearly loved children
- ➢ We are God's workmanship, therefore we live a life of love just as Christ loved us and gave Himself up for us as a fragrant offering and sacrifice to God
- ➢ We live with the fruit of the light, which is all goodness, righteousness, and truth
- ➢ We have nothing to do with the fruitless deeds of darkness
- ➢ We are careful how we live and make the most of every opportunity to love
- ➢ We are filled with the Spirit of God and give thanks to Him for everything in the name of Jesus Christ
- ➢ Wives submit to husbands as unto the Lord
- ➢ Children submit to parents
- ➢ Slaves (employees) submit to masters (employers) with respect as we would obey Christ
- ➢ We do this daily and go from glory to glory
- ➢ We live a life worthy of the calling we have received in Christ Jesus
- ➢ We live a life pleasing to God

The Standards of Christian Conduct

HANDOUT # 5 - HOW MUCH DO YOU KNOW ABOUT JESUS?
(Trivia Challenge)

I. <u>QUESTIONS</u>

1. What does the name Jesus mean?
2. *Jesus* is the Greek form of what English word?
3. Jesus is called _____ which means "God with us"
4. Jesus is also called the _____ which means "The Anointed One"
5. What is the Hebrew word for Christ?
6. Where was Jesus born?
7. Where did Jesus and his family live?
8. What was Jesus' mother's name?
9. Jesus was thought to be the son of what earthly man?
10. Who was actually Jesus' father?
11. What two things happened to the Lord on the 8th day after His birth?
12. What king was disturbed when he heard that Jesus was the one who was born King of the Jews? He later gave orders to kill all the boys in Bethlehem and its vicinity who were two years old and under.
13. In what country and on what continent did Jesus live until the death of Herod?
14. How old was Jesus when he was found in the temple courts sitting among the teachers, listening to them and asking them questions? How long was Jesus missing before He was found?
15. About how old was Jesus when he began His ministry?
16. Who baptized Jesus?
17. After Jesus was baptized, He was led into the desert to be tempted by the devil. He fasted for how long?
18. How many men did Jesus appoint, designating them apostles? Were these the only disciples of Jesus?
19. Name at least 6 of Jesus' designated apostles.
20. Which apostle betrayed Jesus and became a traitor?
21. What new command did Jesus give his disciples?
22. At what place was Jesus crucified?
23. What time was Jesus crucified?
24. Why were Jesus' bones not broken after He was crucified?
25. People refer to Jesus as the Prince of Peace, the Lion of Judah, etc; how did Jesus refer to himself?
26. True or False - Jesus knew, before it happened, that He was going to die and be raised to life on the third day.

HOW MUCH DO YOU KNOW ABOUT JESUS? TRIVIA CHALLENGE

II. ANSWERS

1. The Lord saves
2. Joshua
3. Immanuel (Matthew 1:23)
4. Christ (Matthew 1:16)
5. Messiah
6. Bethlehem in Judea (Matthew 2:1)
7. Nazareth (Luke 2:39)
8. Mary (Matthew 1:18)
9. Joseph (Luke 3:23)
10. God (Matthew 3:16-17; 16:16)
11. He was circumcised and named Jesus (Luke 2:21)
12. King Herod (Matthew 2:1-3; 16)
13. Egypt in Northeast Africa (Matthew 2:14-15)
14. Twelve; 3 days (Luke 2:41-46)
15. Thirty (Luke 3:23)
16. John the Baptist (Matthew 3:13-15)
17. Forty days and forty nights (Matthew 4:2)
18. Twelve (Mark 3:13-19); no there were many disciples (Luke 6:13)
19. Peter, James, John, Andrew, Philip, Bartholomew, Matthew, Thomas, James son of Alphaeus, Thaddaeus also called Judas (son of James), Simon the Zealot, and Judas Iscariot. (Mark 3:14-19; Luke 6:12-16)
20. Judas Iscariot (Luke 6:16; Matthew 10:4)
21. To love one another as He has loved them (John 15:12)
22. Golgotha (place of the skull - Mark 15:22-24)
23. The third hour (Mark 15:25)
24. They found that He was already dead/to fulfill scripture (John 19:31-34 and 36)
25. The Son of Man (Matthew 20:18)
26. True (Matthew 20:17-19)

HANDOUT # 6 - UNDERSTANDING THE MIND

A. BACKGROUND

1. The mind is only going to follow the instructions it understands. We get instructions (or information) from three different sources:

   - The Holy Spirit (Representing the Kingdom of God)
   - Satan (Representing the World)
   - Our Five Senses

2. All three may provide thoughts at the same time, and although our minds can receive an abundance of thoughts and information at the same time, it can only process one set of instructions at a time; thereby making us do what it has received, assimilated, and understood.

3. If the mind has not understood a set of instructions, it is thrown into confusion and immobilization results. If confusion lasts too long, protective devices kick in - rejection, rebellion or total shut down. Emotions flare - depression, anxiety, anger, and hostility.

4. We will reject and hate what we do not understand. We will eventually rebel against it.

5. We will act on what we know and understand.

B. BREAKING THROUGH THE CONFUSION

1. There are 3 things necessary for understanding:

   - Time
   - The desire to understand
   - Instructions

   a) <u>Time</u>

   1. Given to us each day that we are able to open our eyes and rise out of bed. If we are alive, we have time.

2. We are given a new proportion (allotment) of time each day that we awake.

b) <u>Desire to Understand</u>

1. A must!
2. No desire to understand- no understanding.
3. Must accept what is being offered. Accept that these instructions are here for my understanding, and I can understand if I choose to understand or believe I can understand, knowing that it is for my good. (Proverbs chapter 2)

Note: Not many miracles were done in Jesus' hometown because the people thought that they knew Him and rejected His ability and desire to help. They did not understand and, therefore, could not believe that He could work miracles.

4. The opposite of rejection is acceptance (trust).

c) <u>Instructions (The Holy Bible is a good example)</u>

1. Just reading over instructions once does not allow us to understand in most situations. We must read over the instructions more than once to get a good understanding of them. We would want to read over the instructions again, or at least we know we must read over them again, study them, meditate on them, and absorb them, in order to past the test.
2. To get a good understanding of the instructions, more than "cramming" before the test is necessary.
3. Just reading words is hard on the mind sometimes, especially if the subject matter is complicated or deep thought is necessary. There are two good tools that can be used to facilitate the understanding of instructions:

- Illustrations (pictures)

The mind can easily assimilate pictures, visions, etc.

- Examples

The mind can easily understand complicated instructions by an example of what is being stated.
Metaphors help (Isaiah 55:10 - 11)

> When our mind is fixed, our heart is fixed, and out of the abundance of the heart, the mouth speaks.

C. SCRIPTURES RELATING TO THE MIND

1) "… I am He who searches hearts and <u>minds</u>. And I will repay each of you according to your deeds." Revelation 2:23 (NIV)

2) … To put off your old self, and be renewed in the attitude of your <u>minds.</u> Ephesians 4:23 (NIV)

3) Do not be conformed to this world, but be transformed by the renewing of your <u>mind</u>. Romans 12:2 (NIV)

— D. Duncan

HANDOUT # 7 - SELF INVENTORY

In order to change our circumstances and our outward situation, we must first change ourselves inwardly. Take an inventory of what is in you and in your soul for an honest and truthful look at yourself and your ways. Is there anything in you that should not be? How do you know unless you look within yourself to see what's there? Then you will know what to pray about and you can ask the Lord to remove those traits, habits, attitudes, and thoughts that should not be. Ask yourself these questions regularly and pray about the issues that come to light.

ISSUE	Y/N	%Resolved 1-4
Have I spent regular quality time with God?		
Do I thank and praise God daily?		
Have I given God my time, talent and tenth?		
Am I sensitive to the Spirit of God?		
Have I hardened my heart on anything He has told me to do or say?		
Am I indulging in any kind of impurity?		
Do I have any deceitful desires in my heart, causing my heart to be corrupted?		
Do I have any negative attitudes that are not of God about anyone or anything?		
Are my thoughts pure?		
Do I speak truthfully to people?		

ISSUE	Y/N	%Resolved 1-4
Am I angry or enraged with anyone? Have I let the sun go down while I am still angry, giving the devil a foothold?		
In my anger, have I sinned?		
Have I gone to my brother or sister who has sinned against me to resolve the issue just between me and him/her? If the issue is not resolved, have I taken another along or gone to the church about the issue?		
Do I work, doing something useful with my own hands?		
Am I a good steward of what God has given me? Have I returned to Him His share first?		
Have I stolen anything?		
Has any unwholesome talk come out of my mouth (cursing, criticizing, judging, coarse joking, slander)?		
Have I spoken anything to encourage and build up anyone?		
Do I harbor bitterness in my heart?		
Do I have any form of malice in my heart?		
Have I forgiven everyone that has harmed me or has done me wrong?		

ISSUE	Y/N	%Resolved 1-4
Am I kind, compassionate, and loving towards others?		
Do I live in the futility of my own thinking?		
Am I allowing fear to hinder me from who God wants me to be?		
Am I increasing in Godly wisdom and understanding?		
Total Percentage	_____	

Enter a percentage of 1 – 4 in the last column, 4 being completely resolved or accomplished. Add your total percentages from column 3. Strive for 100% resolution.

Ephesians 4
D. Duncan

HANDOUT # 8 - CHARACTER EVALUATION

SITUATION	RESPONSE A	RESPONSE B	CHOICE(A or B)
IN THE HOME			
1. You break your sibling's expensive iPhone without his/her knowledge	Keep quiet hoping they will think someone else did it	Confess your mistake, apologize (ask for forgiveness). Make an agreement to replace or give something of equal value or offer free services to make up for the loss	
2. You lost your job and the bills are behind	Blame your employer, current presidential administration, boss, economy, etc for your loss. Become bitter about your situation and take it out on others.	Pray. Call your creditors to explain the situation and make other arrangements. Have conversations with the family about what happened and what you are willing to do to try to get bills paid (Work at odd jobs, file for unemployment insurance, borrow from family, etc. to pay bills until full time employment is obtained)	
IN THE COMMUNITY			
1. You receive too much change from a cashier	Count it as a blessing from God and keep the change	Return the excess change to the cashier	
2. A police officer gives you a ticket for something you feel was not your fault or you didn't do	Argue with the officer and give him a piece of your mind.	Pray. Calmly discuss your side with the officer. If no agreement is reached, get the officer's name and badge number; if led by the Holy Spirit, take it to court or file an official complaint. If no leading of the Holy Spirit, hold your peace, pay the ticket.	

The Standards of Christian Conduct

SITUATION	RESPONSE A	RESPONSE B	CHOICE (A or B)
3. You are invited to a party, when you arrive you find people are smoking (something bad) and drinking.	Join in the fun!	Tell your friend you have to go and leave. Call your parents or a friend to pick you up if you have no ride, or call a taxi	
ON THE JOB			
1. Your boss gives you a pink slip saying the company is downsizing	Become angry and give your boss a few choice words before leaving. Take it out on someone else.	Pray. Know that God will provide for you and family. Apply for other jobs or do what's necessary to start your own business by faith.	
2. You are at the end of your 1 hour lunch break and realize you need about 20 more minutes to finish your errand.	Finish what you are doing and sneak back in the office, hoping the boss won't see you	Call your boss to let him/her know you will be late, or return to work and finish errand at the end of the day	
3. You did not get the performance award/promotion you thought you deserved.	Become angry and gossip about the person who did receive the award or about your boss. Slack off on your work.	Pray for peace. If appropriate and Spirit agrees, talk to your boss about why you feel you deserved it (if you want to walk in excellence of spirit, you will keep the matter between you and God and look to Him for your reward).	
4. Co-workers are gossiping about you	Confront them and slam them just like they are doing you; pick a fight or gossip about them too.	Pray. If the Spirit leads, confront them privately to discuss the matter, just between you and them. Let them know that you would appreciate it if they would come to you if they have something against you. If they listen, talk about and resolve issue; forgive them or ask for forgiveness. If they continue in a negative way, or the Spirit does not lead you to talk to them, avoid them and pray for them.	

The Standards of Christian Conduct

SITUATION	RESPONSE A	RESPONSE B	CHOICE (A or B)
5. Your boss asks you to meet an unreasonable deadline.	Give your boss a piece to your mind; quit or don't meet the deadline intentionally to show him/her! Grumble and complain about the job.	Give facts (not excuses) about why deadline cannot be met. Offer honest alternative plan to get the job done (say, "this is what I can do by this date").	
6. You have the choice of being late for work or not going at all	Stay home because you are late anyway and the boss is just going to get on your case about it	Call your employer to let them know you will be late and are coming in as soon as possible or let them know you cannot make it in today for a legitimate reason.	
IN THE CHURCH			
1. You felt you were overlooked when leaders were chosen	Change church membership. Gossip about the ministry and why it is not prospering.	Know that God's eyes are still on you even if you must wait another season. Continue to work prayerfully and diligently in the ministry until God moves you because, after all this is between you and God, not you and man.	
2. A member sins against you. You know it is morally wrong and a sin.	Go and tell another member and discuss it. Get them back for what they did.	Pray, then if appropriate based on your prayer, go to him/her and show his fault just between the two of you, take another believer if they do not listen, then to church leadership if they still do not listen. Have nothing to do with them if they do not listen to the church.	
IN SCHOOL			
1. Your classmate wants you to skip school and take a ride with him/her. You know he/she is up to no good.	You take him/her up on the offer. After all, your homework is done and you deserve a break from classes today.	You explain that you would rather go to class and go your own way.	
2. During lunch break, your friends begin to gossip about another friend.	Get the juicy details and tell what you know	Excuse yourself	
TOTAL "A" CHOICES	----------------------------	----------------------------	
TOTAL "B" CHOICES	----------------------------	----------------------------	

If your choices are mostly B, you are a person of integrity and character. Continue to work on making right choices.

If your choices are mostly A, you will definitely benefit from learning how to handle yourself better in different situations. Continue to read your Bible and learn from Jesus' example how to conduct yourself.

D. Duncan

HANDOUT # 9 - <u>I POSITIVELY AFFIRM THE FOLLOWING:</u>

I BELIEVE GOD. I BELIEVE HE IS WORKING IN ME NO MATTER WHAT I MAY FEEL OR HOW THE SITUATION MAY LOOK. THE LORD HAS BEGUN A GOOD WORK IN ME, AND HE WILL BRING IT TO COMPLETION. (PHIL 2:13; 1:6)

I AM FREE FROM CONDEMNATION WHEN I MAKE A MISTAKE. I HAVE NOT REACHED MY GOAL, BUT I PRESS TOWARD THE MARK FOR THE PRIZE OF MY HIGHER CALLING OF GOD IN CHRIST. (PHIL 3:13)

I FORGET THOSE THINGS WHICH ARE BEHIND ME; AND REACH FOR THOSE THINGS WHICH ARE BEFORE ME. AND IF ON SOME POINT I THINK DIFFERENTLY, THAT TOO GOD WILL MAKE CLEAR TO ME. (PHIL 3:13, 15)

I AM FREE FROM FEAR AND GUILT FOR GOD HAS GIVEN ME THE SPIRIT OF LOVE AND OF POWER AND OF A SOUND MIND. I ACCEPT THE LORD'S GIFT OF LOVE AND POWER AND SOUNDNESS OF MIND. (II TIMOTHY 1:7)

I AM A NEW CREATURE IN MY LIFE WITH CHRIST. OLD THOUGHTS, FEELINGS, LIMITATIONS, FEARS, SICKNESS, DISEASE, LONELINESS, FATIGUE, STUBBORNNESS ARE PASSED AWAY. EVERYTHING IS NEW! NEW MIND NEW BODY, NEW SOUL, NEW SPIRIT.

I LOVE THE LORD MY GOD WITH ALL MY HEART, WITH ALL MY MIND, AND WITH ALL MY SOUL. I LOVE MY NEIGHBOR AS I LOVE MYSELF, AND I LOVE MYSELF AS CHRIST LOVES ME.

I AM FREE TO ENJOY LIFE! I DO ENJOY LIFE AND SEE THE GOOD THINGS IN LIFE AND PEOPLE. I AM NOT A COMPLAINER.

I FEEL STRONG AND POWERFUL AS I TAKE POSSESSION OF MY WILL AND SUBMIT IT TO GOD'S WILL.

I AM FREE TO LIVE AND LOVE AS A TRUE MAN/WOMAN OF GOD. I UNDERSTAND MY VALUE AS A GODLY MAN/WOMAN AND I USE MY GOD-GIVEN TALENTS TO HELP OTHERS.

I MAKE THE MOST OF MY TIME EACH DAY. I DO NOT WASTE TIME.

I AM NOT A PROCRASTINATOR. I AM A "DO IT NOW" PERSON AND I MAKE MY ALLOTMENT OF TIME SERVE GOD.

I AM EAGER TO GET UP IN THE MORNING AND GET INTO ACTION EVERYDAY.

I AM DEEPLY FULFILLED AS I WALK IN GOD'S WISDOM AND DIVINE GUIDANCE.

I FEEL STRONG AND POWERFUL AS GOD GIVES ME CONSISTENT STRENGTH AND WISDOM TO OPERATE IN HIS PURPOSE FOR ME IN MY LIFE.

I AM THANKFUL AND VERY GRATEFUL FOR THE LONG, FULFILLING AND PROSPEROUS LIFE THAT GOD HAS GIVEN ME.

GOD HAS REDEEMED THE TIME THAT WAS LOST WHILE I WAS IN THE WILDERNESS. I AM TRULY GRATEFUL TO MY FATHER FOR ALL HIS MANY BLESSINGS.

I AM SET FREE FROM NEGATIVISM, GUILT AND SHAME. I AM AWARE THAT I AM LOVED.

I AM THANKFUL TO GOD, FOR HE HAS PROVIDED ME WITH VIBRANT HEALTH AND ENERGY WHICH I USE EACH DAY TO CARRY OUT HIS STATUTES AND COMMANDS.

I AM STRONG IN MY CONVICTIONS AND I CANNOT BE SWAYED. I AM NOT ASHAMED OF THE GOSPEL OF JESUS CHRIST, FOR IT IS THE POWER UNTO SALVATION.

I TRUST IN THE LORD WITH ALL MY HEART AND I DO NOT LEAN TO MY OWN UNDERSTANDING. IN ALL MY WAYS I ACKNOWLEDGE HIM, AND HE DIRECTS MY PATHS. (PROV 3:5-6)

I HAVE NO OTHER gods OR idols BEFORE GOD.

I CAST DOWN IMAGINATIONS AND EVERY HIGH THING THAT EXHALTETH ITSELF AGAINST THE KNOWLEDGE OF GOD. I BRING INTO

CAPTIVITY EVERY THOUGHT TO THE OBEDIENCE OF CHRIST. (2 CORINTHIANS 10:5).

I UNDERSTAND THAT GOD IS MOULDING ME AND PREPARING ME AND MAKING ME INTO ONE GREATLY USED BY HIM. I FEEL STRONGER EVERY DAY AS I POSITION MYSELF TO RECEIVE HIS BLESSINGS.

I AM A PART OF THE FELLOWSHIP OF GOD.

LORD, I BELIEVE!

HANDOUT # 10 - **SELF EVALUATION OF MERCY AND HUMILITY**

SERVICE	Yes	No	Total Points
In the last year I visited a sick believer or non-believer			
In the last year I visited the jail to encourage an/the inmate(s)			
In the last year I spent quality time with the elderly			
In the last year I invited a child without a father present in his/her life to an event			
In the last year I helped a widow or single mother			
In the last year I gave to help the homeless or poor			
In the last year I helped feed the hungry			
In the last year I volunteered my time in the community			
In the last year I invited an underprivileged person to dinner			
In the last two months I called and checked on a fellow believer			
In the last year I contributed to a charitable cause (other than my church)			
In the last two days I prayed for someone other than myself or my family			
In the last year I witnessed to a non-believer			
GRAND TOTAL	-----	----	

INSTRUCTIONS:

Check "Yes" or "No" to each statement.

For every "Yes" answer give yourself 2 points (write 2 in the total points column).

For every "No" answer give yourself "0" points (write 0 in the total points column).

For each statement you should have a 0 or 2 in the Total Points column.

Enter your "grand total" in the last row from the total points column. The highest possible score is 26.

RESULTS:

If you scored 18-26, you show mercy with humility in your walk with God regularly. You are storing treasures in heaven, and will be rewarded for your acts of kindness and humility.

If you scored 10-16, you are merciful toward your fellow man; continue to strive towards greater levels of mercy and humility. You have treasures in heaven; continue to accumulate them.

If you scored 2-8, you could benefit from practicing more mercy. Ask the Lord to show you how to be more merciful toward your fellow man. Evaluate yourself again in a year.

HANDOUT # 11 - <u>GROWING IN THE WORD</u>

I. BACKGROUND

When we decide to live for Christ, we are in essence deciding to live according to the "Word," who is Christ (John 1:1 – In the beginning was the Word and the Word was with God, and the Word was God… and the Word was made flesh and dwelt among us).

The Word of God is the Bible. When we experience the Bible, we experience Christ; we decide to live according to the principles and instructions outlined in the Bible. When we grow in the "Word," we grow in Christ.

II. STAGES OF GROWTH

Growing up does not happen overnight. There are stages of growth and there are lessons to be learned along the way. As we mature, the lessons are different and the tests or trials become more difficult. If a person is to grow, he/she must not give up, but persevere through the tests and trials as they become more and more challenging and as time goes on. One day, however, the lessons and the tests and the persevering through them will pay off and we will be glad we went through what we went through in order to have what we have. This describes growing and maturing as a Christian. We can compare it with growing up and going to school. Let's look at the different stages of growth:

A. NEWBORN

A newborn baby comes into the world knowing nothing. It depends on its parents for everything. It has just arrived and is accepted into the family. This is like a person who has just accepted Christ and has decided to live for Him. He has heard the Word and accepted the call to live for Jesus Christ. He is accepted into the family of Believers.

HTW (hear the Word) > ATC (accept the call)

B. INFANT

An infant has not only heard the Word and accepted the call, but craves spiritual milk. They go to church and try to learn all they can about their new found life.

HTW > ATC > CSM (**crave spiritual milk**)

C. TODDLER

A toddler not only does the above, but is also filled with the wonder of the Word and its truths. They are learning to walk in the Word and want to tell everyone about what they know.

HTW > ATC > CSM > FWW (**filled with wonder**)

D. PRESCHOOLER

A preschooler does the above and prepares for the tests.

HTW>ATC>CSM>FWW>PFT (**prepare for tests**)

E. KINDERGARTEN

Once a person gets to kindergarten, he/she has heard the Word (HTW), accepted the call (ATC), craved Spiritual milk (CSM), has been filled with wonder (FWW), has prepared for the test (PFT) and they face the class and the teacher (FTC & T).

HTW> ATC >CSM > FWW > PFT > FTC & T (**face the class and teacher**)

F. ELEMENTARY SCHOOL

In elementary school, the student has a little more of a challenge. He not only does the above, but takes the tests and learns his lessons.

HTW > ATC >CSM > FWW > PFT > FTC & T > TTT & LYL (**take the tests and learn your lesson**)

G. MIDDLE SCHOOL

Middle school students do the above and grow in grace and knowledge.

HTW > ATC > CSM > FWW > PFT > FTC & T > TTT & LYL > GIG & K **(grow in grace and knowledge)**

H. HIGH SCHOOL

High school students have graduated to a higher level. They do the above, learn obedience and mature in Spirit.

HTW > ATC > CSM > FWW > PFT > FTC & T > TTT & LYL > GIG & K > LO & MIS **(learn obedience and mature in Spirit)**

I. COLLEGE

College students have learned a lot. By this time many tests have been taken, homework has been done, and lessons have been learned. At this level, the student learns and has little problem with dying to self.

HTW > ATC > CSM > FWW > PFT > FTC &T > TTT & LYL > GIG & K > LO & MIS > DTS **(die to self)**

J. GRAD SCHOOL

The student has matured tremendously by this time and can face many challenges with ease. He/she has died to self and is living for Christ. Not only that, but he/she is living the Word, not just hearing it and talking about it.

HTW > ATC > CSM > FWW > PFT > FTC & T > TTT & LYL > GIG & K > LO & MIS > DTS > LTW **(live the Word)**

K. PHD

A PHD not only does the above, but has come to the point where he/she is living the life and can teach others to do the same by ministering the Word.

HTW > ATC > CSM > FWW > PFT > FTC & T > TTT & LYL > GIG & K > LO & MIS > DTS > LTW > MTW (**minister the Word**)

Evaluate where you are in your spiritual growth. At what stage do you find yourself? Be honest and do not be ashamed; as long as we keep moving and growing, we will get the diplomas, certificates, degrees, and awards our time and labor deserve. Just stay in school (the race) and finish your course!

D. Duncan

CPSIA information can be obtained at www.ICGtesting.com
Printed in the USA
LVOW031929050812

292913LV00002B/3/P